from

Fortress

to

Freedom

Deborah L. W. Roszel

Torchflame Books
An imprint of Light Messages

From Fortress to Freedom
Deborah L.W. Roszel
www.fortresstofreedom.com
info@deborahroszel.com

Published 2014, by Torchflame Books
    an Imprint of Light Messages
www.lightmessages.com
Durham, NC 27713 USA

Paperback ISBN: 978-1-61153-121-3
Ebook ISBN: 978-1-61153-122-0

All Scripture quotations, unless otherwise noted, are taken from the New International Version of the Bible, Copyright © 1973, 1978, 1984 Biblica. Used by permission. All rights reserved worldwide.

This book is dedicated
to the remarkable men
who helped me to realize that
I am a remarkable woman.

Contents

Pain on Purpose
(an Introduction)

*H*ow great indeed is the love the Father has shown toward us; how excellent are His mercies, beyond measure.

He watched over me, carefully sheltering me, leading me only as quickly as I could follow. He chose me long before I was ever to choose Him and He directed me in diverse ways toward His path, the only way to joy.

When I was a child, I thought as a child, even though I did not think as other children. I was unusual (my grandmother's word in describing my specialness), and I did not see as a child, but much more clearly and sharply than the knowledge of my few years could explain.

And my Lord, Who knew me and formed me and chose me before my mother knew of me, smiled down upon me in pure and absolute love.

Love was all I longed for. In seeing as I did, I saw the lonely, empty spaces behind the eyes of those around me and I knew that within me there was an emptiness aching to be filled. This was the need for God, of course, but I did not realize it.

I was only a child. I thought as a child. Although I saw some of the truth of the human condition, some of the pain of separation from God, some of the ancient loss Adam suffered for his disobedience, I did not know how to respond to the vast emptiness in and around me. It seemed that the answer had something to do with being good, but I was unsure.

I longed to know. I yearned to understand. Perhaps somehow I thought that if I paid attention, if I took notes and studied, I would sooner or later unlock the secret answer that would relieve the misery of being alone.

I remember quite clearly thinking that I wanted my mother to sit still for a day, for an entire day, and answer my questions. I was five or six, and the things I knew I didn't know seemed endless to me. I was sure my mother would know and share the answers if I could just have enough of her time to ask.

She didn't understand, but that does not mean she did not care. She showed her love for her family by doing things – cooking, shopping, saving, sewing, mending, canning, freezing, cleaning – always cleaning. Always cleaning. Still.

She loved me the best way she knew. She answered my endless questions as I followed her through my world, watching her clean. She didn't need to read to me any more, since I had learned so long ago, but she helped me find good things to read. Gradually I found that the answers I sought were more readily available from books, even old, faded, dusty ones, than from my young, pretty, clean mother. I could lose myself and find myself in a library.

So impersonal books replaced the warmth of connection, of relationship, of personhood. I could learn, and that became my consuming passion.

Still my Eternal Friend watched over me. Still He wanted to fill me with joy, but His heart was saddened as He watched me stepping away from it. He could see a dire future for me, as I had closed my heart against the pain of watching my father leave for a year on an overseas military assignment; as I had tried to be the adult companion I thought my mother must have needed while we waited for my father's return; and as I denied yet another part of myself, turning to study rather than to relationship to quench my thirst for understanding.

At six years old, my future was no longer bright.

We live in a fallen world, but it is fallen by our own choice. Christ came and lived as if the world did not have to be a sinful place; at any point He could have chosen sin, for He was tempted in all ways as we are. But He did not sin. We, however, apart from Christ, do not easily choose to keep from sinning. And with each sin we lose a bit of the clarity of vision, a bit of the hope for reward, a bit of the confidence to stand where we know it is right to stand.

The pattern of my choices, even made in the innocence of childhood, was becoming a path toward darkness and away from Light. My vision was growing cloudy, my hope was waning, my confidence weakening. And God intervened.

He did something that He had not done until that point in my life. He allowed me to be hurt.

As His chosen, we know that everything that comes to us in life is first sifted through His hands of love. Everything. God allowed me to be hurt so that I would see that I was worthy, worth loving, worth saving. I had begun, even at this tender age, to believe I was not. My father had left me: I knew in my mind that he was not to be gone forever, but one year in a life of six years is a very long time, and in my heart I felt abandoned. My mother did not want me: I knew that was not true, but she was too busy to spend time with me, and no matter how clean I stayed, how correctly I behaved, I could not be a part of her.

God looked on this beautiful family and saw the unavoidable hurt that we caused one another. He saw that I would be lost if I did not fight. So He gave me a reason to fight: an experience that changed me forever.

The fear and pain and anger that came as a result of my sexual abuse were like an ocean of cold water into which I was suddenly thrown, but against which I struggled and fought just as a drowning person would have. I went into survival mode, just as God knew I would, and all my instincts of self-preservation, instincts God had given me when He made me, took over to run my shattered life.

But my life was not shattered. The impressions that I was damaged, and that the world was dangerous, and that people were untrustworthy, were all things that I needed to know. I needed this knowledge to be able to protect myself as I navigated the troubled waters of adolescence and the even more turbulent seas of young adulthood. I also needed the fear and the certainty of my inability to save myself, in order to begin to acknowledge my need for Christ. My very competence in coping, my security in knowledge, would have kept me from seeking, and certainly from accepting, salvation and ultimate healing.

God's ways are not man's ways and they do not always hold up to our version of scrutiny. As surely as I know that God loves me, though, I know that nothing happens to me apart from His love and nothing ever has. He alone stands outside of time and is able to see all the possible consequences of our actions, to anticipate the endings of the stories we write by our decisions. He alone is qualified and capable of intervening to provide opportunities for us to correct our course, to give tools for us to cope with unforeseen challenges, to offer support and strength through whatever means He, and only He, knows to be best.

Even pain, then, has a purpose. "And we know that all things work together for good to them that love God, to them who are the called according to his purpose" (Romans 8:28). And I know that my pain worked together with my nature and my life for good to me, because I did and I do love God, and I am undeniably called according to His purpose.

Thank you, Lord.

This book is about God's touch, God's light, God's love, and it is also about pain and healing. I have lived most of my life struggling with depression, self-condemnation, criticism, sarcasm, anger, hopelessness, shame, guilt, and fear. All of this resulted from a single incident of sexual abuse when I was six years old, which I processed all alone and ultimately repressed for roughly thirty years. I thank God for engaged, believing parents who gave me a strong and safe place to grow up, to learn about God's love, to set high standards and work to achieve them.

In January of 2011 God used a single remark from a friend to start a chain reaction that completely changed my world, setting me free from bondage that had grown to feel so much a part of me that I'd forgotten I was in chains. I had known for many years that I was living life inside a fortress that I had built to protect myself from hurt. During the weeks that followed God chose to take me out of that dim, gray, cloistered existence and place me where He had intended for me to be all along: in a Garden of His design, lush and vibrant and alive. He showed me the true source of my hurts and granted me healing.

The healing I received touched every area of my life and allowed me to start becoming, at age forty-eight, the person I'd always dreamed I could be but stopped trying to be before I was twenty years old. The writing here chronicles that explosion of light and life and love, not in a scientific or historical way, but in the way of the spirit, with images and analogies and symbols.

As He showed me things, I had an irrepressible need to write what He showed me. I've never been a morning person, but for weeks I woke up at His urging every morning to listen and to write. This book represents roughly the first three months of that work.

Almost as soon as I began writing these notes, which began as letters to a dear friend, I knew that I was also writing to share more broadly, because the healing was not for me alone, but for many of God's beloved children who are suffering just as I was. My fervent prayer since then is that His words, spoken to and through me, will touch and heal many, and that more and more people will join us here, dancing in His Garden.

A Thursday Morning

There's pre-dawn snow, as predicted. It's a pretty traditional Georgia snow: about an inch, soft and wet, mixed with a little ice. And also traditionally Georgian, the temperature is 30 now and headed above freezing before 9:00 a.m. I don't keep up with school closings at our home school, but I imagine this will just qualify for a delayed start, if that; the roads aren't even white.

I'm supposed to be getting up at 8:00, so these moments to write are blessings from God. He wakes me a little before my alarm clock goes off almost every morning, giving me extra time to be with Him. That's been happening frequently since my Peru mission trip three years ago when I learned to recognize and pay attention to His voice – or to be more accurate, to trust myself to believe what I was hearing. He speaks to me in very quiet, affirming tones; He guides, informs, helps, and teaches as often as I will listen. So much I have had to learn about believing in what He's given me! I guess I'm enrolled in His home school of daily lessons.

Ah, the sun's peeking through now, and the trees really do look like a fairyland –the setting for a fantasy wedding photo shoot with a palette of white and silver, pink and peach, backed by the perfect clear blue pastel sky. They'd better shoot fast, because in the time it's taking me to write this, the whole palette is changing. Including the light. The bride's eye shadow will be all wrong in under five minutes. Such pressure!

The light in here is changing as well. God and I have had our quiet visit. Enough talking. Time to go live some more! Here's to another day walking in joy and strength and love.

Morning Musings

Yesterday morning and this, God chose a particularly pleasant alarm clock to wake me for our visit. He sometimes just whispers, sometimes nudges me a little, sometimes lays a hand on my head. Yesterday and today He sent a wren to perch on the porch for morning prayers. I heard the little guy singing and woke up to join in. What a beautiful voice! I hope the songs of my heart are as pleasant to the ears of God as the wren's songs are to mine.

It has always been the desire of my heart to be able to wake up like this, with pure music flowing to and from me, in love and surrounded by love, with joy infused through all my awareness. Could it be possible to move from unconscious bliss, rest from trouble, and timeless existence into fully conscious bliss, rest and life? Rather than waking with an immediate sense of dread or burden or fear, I have longed to wake full of all He created me to be and to have: instead of heaviness, light; instead of chains, freedom; instead of oppression, power; instead of depression, peace.

From birth I had heard, and soon afterward had read for myself, the Bible stories of people who had lived that way. I believed it had been possible once upon a time but was afraid to believe it could still be. I guess I believed it as I had believed in Santa Claus: I knew it was more real than Santa, but I was not able to get past my tiny insignificant self enough to build my life on it.

Thirty or so years ago, as a young woman, I had a glimpse of this life being possible for me as I became aware of myself as a talented and beautiful child of God. Somehow in the bustle and blessing of the intervening years I lost my focus or forgot my position. I knew I was capable, but I hid my lack of confidence behind misunderstandings about submissiveness and obedience. I could not conceive that the stories of the Bible could be true in my own life.

Today, as in recent days, I increasingly see that the stories are all true and their truth is real in my life. Not only do I see it, but I feel it throughout my spirit and my body. The sensation is so real that I occasionally focus on the feeling of my feet touching the ground just to be sure I'm still in the physical world. I am so very glad that God didn't give up on "tiny insignificant me." Instead, He kept holding my hand, giving me increasing confidence to open my eyes more often and for longer periods. Now, at last, I can look as long as I like with eyes wide, unblinking.

Changes

*H*ow quickly the world changes, even in just a few days. The sun is coming up noticeably earlier than when I started writing each morning. Every day God's hand shows us the morning. Beautiful in itself, each day is even more lovely when seen as part of His plan to bring light and life to the world in twenty-four-hour installments.

Of course, I'm changing also.

The changes in me seem to have happened quickly, but that's only because I'm just now seeing them in the dawn of each spiritual morning. The light is a little different each day, and I see more of the path each morning; I'm able to walk in the light ever more consciously and confidently.

In my new day with the Lord, I find myself doing things alone with Him more and more. He's been making me more independent, and for the past year at least I have been fully aware of His doing so, of His reminding me that I don't need anyone else to decide things or do things for me, that He and I together can do life just fine.

I still don't know for sure where this independence will take me. It is not pushing me away from anyone or anything, but the tiny daily changes in the light are showing me that I'm heading into new places without physical companions. At the same time, I've never felt less alone than I feel now in this continuous consciousness of Him.

Today's adventure: I'm going to church all by myself. I haven't done that since marriage nearly twenty-six years ago. Six weeks ago this would not have happened, and it couldn't have happened before that, either. But here I go. I wonder what I'll see there in this beautiful morning light.

Morning Perspective

I've never been a morning person. I am philosophically in favor of being up in the early morning but constitutionally challenged when faced with the choice of getting out of bed or, well, staying put. I've always been slow to wake up, even after leaving the bliss of repose; my focus and attention and attitude tend not to be lined up with my will until very late in the mornings.

Until recently.

Many of the most memorable moments in my life have happened at daybreak. I wonder if the reason I'm such a pertinacious night owl is that I'm pressing toward the dawn. Several of the mileposts in my life are colored by sunrise. Mornings by the ocean, in particular: a frolic with my sister when I was around sixteen, she seven; the last morning at Governor's School down by the Battery in Charleston; a run with my oldest son one summer when we were all in Charleston; a long stroll with my third son last summer. And of course all these mornings that God has been waking me while the house is quiet, while I'm already still and He doesn't have to still me so that I may know He is God. The little grey cells seem to be particularly absorbent in the early morning, too, so I remember the things I realize at this time of day. There are fewer extraneous stimuli to get absorbed alongside, perhaps. An Oriental minimalist approach to the situation—less really is more—rather than the more American mindset of overindulgence. It fascinates me to see the different ways we humans think in different parts of the world.

I've often thought it no accident that God chose to come to earth in the geographical center of philosophical divergence. A few steps from the cross, in any direction, takes one to a particular way of viewing the world that doesn't line up with any of the other views but seems all-encompassing and complete with only a few tiny cracks that hardly mar it: a decent way of looking at life. Unless one steps back to the cross and looks again. Then it's obvious that those worldview cracks are anything but tiny; they are gaping chasms into which souls are falling one after another. No wonder Jesus wept when He stood looking over Jerusalem.

Thank you, Lord, for setting foot on this earth, Your earth. Thank you for showing us the way to live, from early to late, from East to West, from beginning to end. Thank you for being God and helping us to know so. Amen.

Tears and Chocolate

I'm feeling cozy and comfy this morning in my fuzzy pink bathrobe. Starting to notice that it fits differently, too. I haven't written yet about one particular side effect of my new exercise program, walking in joy. I've lost, so far, thirteen pounds in the month since all this started, completely as a secondary result of this new way of being.

I've known for, I don't know, always, that food and drink have been for me a substitute, an idol of sorts. I've turned to chocolate and to diet soda in particular to soothe and strengthen and comfort and sustain me. I've done it consciously, even, making mental deals with myself or with God, deliberately rationalizing. I've denied myself the pleasures, but I've always gone back. I've tried cutting back but always increased my "using" again. For the most part, I'd settled into a sort of adulterous compromise: God is what I really need, and He's there, but He knows I'm weak and He won't begrudge me this bit of pleasure. I mean, He made me, He knows me, and it's not like I'm doing something really bad. He made chocolate too, right? And He wants us to enjoy our lives?

As I wrote those words, it occurred to me that, in spite of the fact that my prayers tend to be most often prayers of thanksgiving for God's provision and care –

I have never bowed my head and thanked God for chocolate before grabbing it to "meet my need." Nor have I thanked him for the "strength" I find in a Diet Dr. Pepper.

Ouch.

So much for the bathrobe. I'm standing naked before God now.

(Pausing to breathe and to bow, to repent and to receive . . .)

I'm free! (That is in the sense of being available, and also in the sense of being delivered.) Wow! That just happened. How many more doors is God going to open, how many more prison cells is He going to unlock and lead me out of? I mean, seriously, the pile of chains in my wake is getting pretty substantial. Hallelujah!

Very little in my life escapes my spiritual notice. That is not to sound prideful; it's just that I know, as surely as I know there is gravity, that every act of my physical life is a reflection of my spiritual life, and I cannot avoid that fact any more than I can escape gravity. I don't think about gravity every moment, but I also don't ever try to act as if it's not there. So I've been fully aware of my idolatry, though I have been sometimes trying to ignore it, ignore the fact that God has been trying, trying, trying, several times every day for twenty-three years or more, to show me that He could meet my every need. I've known that my idolatry was imprisoning me by my own choice, but I haven't had the will to choose otherwise.

The mystery, the incomprehensibleness of God – we receive all that He gives us by faith, but even the faith itself is a gift from Him. O, the wonder of this, that the God of all creation chooses, deliberately, consciously, all-knowingly chooses to love one such as I. I, who could not even choose to speak the simple word, "Help," and chose instead to try to fill my emptiness with – candy? Soda pop? Really?? My God, if I had only listened.

When my husband and I had been married a little less than a year he took a new job and we moved to a town halfway between his job and mine. The relevant result of that, for this narrative, was that because of the combination of commutes in opposite directions, an unreasonable job description for him, and his workaholism, I spent most of my life alone for a while. I was not ready for it, and I could not escape the fear and grief and loneliness. I can see now, and I knew then, though I could not appropriate the knowledge, that God was there with me; I was not alone. His light was there; it was not dark, though in my memory that year is a year of blackness with only one or two tiny points of light.

I lived with depression as a constant companion from then until February 2007, when I finally took the hand God was offering me, had been offering me all along. I was at a marriage retreat and as a final note, an afterthought in response to an audience question, the speaker said, "If you can ever get your head around how much God loves the person sitting in your chair, it will change your world."

The person sitting . . . in MY chair? My chair, not the one beside me, the person I'm supposed to love, honor and cherish? Not the chair on the other side, the person who is my brother or sister in Christ, whom I am to love and serve and work alongside? My chair. Mine.

Me?

And God whispered, "I want you to walk with me. I have some things to show you. You can't see them while you're taking Paxil, so you can stop taking that now."

And I rose up to walk in newness of life.

I lost forty pounds over the next few months on that walking program.

I gained some of it back during a very tough year for one of my sons, when I relied on the wrong things to get me through all the ugliness of dealing with the school that year.

Now I can't imagine ever NOT relying on God for help in a challenge. He's not there in the sense that "God is always there with you." He's HERE. He is not with me, He is in me, and He has been all along. Being conscious of that now, how can I ever go back? Perish the thought. God forbid it. I know I am weak, but I am not just trusting Him for help in trouble now or for guidance in life. He is my very breath. "Inspiration." "Respiration." "Spirit-filled." They're all the same.

So, I've not really been eating much lately. The occasional transient emptiness of physical hunger reminds me of my need for God, and also of my unending fullness in Him. Food is not something I really seem to need. It is certainly not something that fills me. Feasting on God's Word, now that's filling. As for Diet Dr. Pepper, well – it's a decent drink, but it doesn't quench my thirst or my desire for wholeness. A drink of water and a prayer are much more effective.

The Eyes Have It

I wonder how many women thought they were going to marry Jesus bar-Joseph. I know I would have thought a lot about it.

It's the eyes, mostly. The hands are gentle; the voice is soothing; the body language, the posture – open. They invite me to rest, to be a guest in the presence of this unusual man. But the eyes, the eyes invite me somewhere else.

These are eyes that hold no selfishness. Of course, there is no need for Him to be selfish, as He is complete in Himself, in perfect union with the Father and the Spirit. His self is whole. What a beautiful thought, to be whole in oneself. I want to know more.

These are eyes of mercy. They see my most inward pain, acknowledge it, and gently touch it. But the touch does not bring with it any discomfort; it is a healing touch. He bathes my wounds – the hurts no one can see – with His tears, cleanses them of all impurity, and leaves them with a mother's kiss that heals the boo-boo completely. A boo-boo. My heart, ripped open by selfish, greedy, lustful acts that left me torn and bleeding emotionally if not physically – that damaged heart I pieced together alone in the dark just to stay alive – that heart, He sees and heals as easily as I put a band-aid on my child's almost invisible scrape and, with a kiss and a prayer, send her off to partake of more of life.

Most of all, these are eyes filled with unconditional love. I've never seen it before. Perhaps the shadows in my own eyes, the shades I've put there for protection, have kept me from seeing it in other eyes. I can't think about that now, because the beauty of that love, burning in that heart, visible in those eyes, is too entrancing. I can't look away from the flame. I close my own eyes, but still I see it. He sees me. He sees me entirely, in space and time, with no shade, no covering to shield me from His gaze. He sees all of me, all at once, and accepts it all.

The intimacy of the moment, the union and communion, is so real that my body responds as if flesh had met flesh. This is too wonderful, too ecstatic. This is why someone would willingly throw herself into the flames for love. But He knows even this, since He created me. He knows I would respond in this way, and the soothing voice calls me back, the gentle hands lift me and place me back where I began, where I first caught His eye, a safe distance from the flame.

He kisses me on the forehead and sends me out to partake of more of life.

Good Morning, Moon

J tried, I really did, to stay in bed last night/this morning. I didn't go upstairs until 3:00. But the moon was so beautiful, so radiant, its light so sacred, that I couldn't go to sleep. I kept opening my eyes and looking at the light and smiling. And then at 5:30 my husband, and then my youngest son, got up troubled; since I was awake anyway, I went to check on them. The (diabetic) husband had low blood sugar and a snack fixed that; the son had some mysterious pains in his feet that I couldn't figure out or fix, so he and I curled up on the sofa for warmth and comfort. I finally dozed off around 6:30.

So when I blinked at 7:25, smiled at the morning light, then remembered the short night, I really did try to close my eyes again. But how can I close my eyes with that Face smiling at me? Heading to the kitchen, thinking maybe this day I'd start with a diet soda, I passed the cabinet for glasses and filled up with water instead. Ah, what a life. Joy!

The sacred light last night reminded me of a vision I had years back. I could see a space, an open place that was lit from an invisible source. The light was everywhere and nowhere, clear but not really bright. Much like last night's moonlight minus the beautiful black shadows.

It always fills me with wonder, realizing that the moon is only reflecting the light of the sun. It always gives me pause, remembering that we are to reflect God's light to the world in the same way.

I wonder if heaven, where neither sun nor moon is needed for light, is lit by the glory of God reflecting off our faces.

"The Son is the radiance of God's glory" (Hebrews 1:3).

Way cool. I'd like to be that.

The Morning After

*G*ood morning, Lord.

This morning the words on my heart as I wake up are my words, a prayer. Some mornings I don't know whose words they are, mine or God's. I acknowledge that the words I think of as mine, if they hold any truth or goodness, are from Him. This morning's words come from my broken and contrite heart, regardless of how they got there.

Dearest, most precious Father, I am overcome. The lushness, the excessiveness of Your love excites a passion in me like none I have ever known. I will no longer describe myself as a timid, frightened girl, Lord, but for so many years I lived as one; I am challenged to be in the presence of so much that my heart has always desired.

The little girl inside of me, the one who hid so long ago, was not afraid to play in Your Garden. She trusted You completely and believed that all You had made was good. She mistakenly believed that everyone You made heard You as she did, loved as she did, cherished as she did. When that mistaken belief was shattered, she built strong walls to protect herself from those who did not love as You love. As she grew taller, she built the walls taller; as she gained strength, she chose larger and heavier stones to place around her, leaving only enough space for air and the sliver of sunshine that smiled through the cracks as You passed by on Your constant watch.

For You, yes You, were there on patrol: my own personal bodyguard, spiritguard, my constant sentinel, walking back and forth in our Garden, the one You made for me, protecting my fortress, the one I thought I had to build. Protecting me. Thank you, my Captain, that You never left me, even when I unintentionally left You.

I could no longer see the Garden. I could no longer smell its sweetness. I could faintly hear the music of its songs, and there was the regular sliver of sunlight that shone upon my cold, gray, stone floor. I knew the Garden was there, but I knew there was great and grave danger there as well. Occasionally I would pick at the walls from the inside; once in a while I could widen a crack.

When You died for me on that black and sunless morning, the earth shook. That earthquake, that shuddering of Your creation under the weight of sin You bore for me, prefigured the final shaking off of the chains of that sin. That earthquake shook the foundations, the very ground on which I had placed my cold, gray stones so that even through the floor I could not be hurt in my fortress.

Thank you, Lord, for reaching into the pile of rubble I thought was a castle, gradually lifting the stones so that the light would not blind me and slowly, slowly bringing me to my feet to stand once again in Your Garden. Our Garden, the one You made for me and placed me in.

Overwhelmed this morning with all the messages my holy senses (made holy by You) are bringing to me, all the love I am experiencing and acknowledging, I begin to feel, well, tipsy. And then I find myself feeling very, very sober.

Oh, God, in Your infinite mercy, please, please do not let me fall. I don't feel weak, not with You here, but I know that others have fallen in this Garden. Others have succumbed to its lushness and beauty and delight and have forgotten that even in all its passionate excess it is only a dim reflection of You and of what You want us to have with You. Let me not drink, Lord, if I am going to drink too deeply. I choose to be with You, to walk with You in this Garden, but I would choose to go back to my rubble rather than make a single step that would cloud the clear and shining love in Your eyes.

Amen.

Van Gogh

The clouds gave way about the time I went to bed. So as I lay down in the dark, it ceased to be dark. Again. I adjusted the blinds to let the light in – the same blinds I had just closed getting ready for bed. My still-awake husband chuckled as I hopped out of bed, darted to the window, and adjusted the view. It didn't keep me up all night this time, but it was such a nice surprise that we were both quite awake for quite some time.

It's always been pretty easy for me to fall asleep in any light. It has been interesting to see how awake I can become in the presence of God's light, or in this case, His moonlight. This morning when I woke up smiling in His sunlight, I thought of Vincent van Gogh.

Van Gogh's story touched me when I studied his life as part of high school French class. I felt an affinity for his sensitivity, and curiosity about the proposed link between manic-depressive illness and creativity. Of course, I've loved his paintings ever since, for their color and movement and pain and beauty and power. He's one of the reasons I want to go to Paris – to see his paintings – before going on to the southern part of France where he did so much of his work.

Once, I got to see an original at the High Museum in Atlanta. Do you know I can't even remember what painting it was? What I do remember is breathing. Standing in front of the canvas, as close as security would allow and I would dare, simply gazing and breathing, imagining the master standing there creating this one stroke at a time, pausing to choose the color that would bring his next object to life. The other art consumers in the gallery looked with more or less brief pauses and moved on. But I don't think they saw.

I was less a consumer and more a communicant in that moment. In the same way that I imagine being at the table with Christ in communion, taking the bread from His hand, drinking the cup He will drink, I stood in worship in front of this painting, imagining, hoping that I could possibly be breathing maybe one molecule of air that van Gogh had breathed. I hope it wasn't sacrilegious; my heart was drawn to the beauty and the pain, just as it is drawn to Christ. In the light of my recent experiences, I can say that I trust it was God using my senses, my mind, my heart, to speak to me about Himself.

One of the many things God wanted me to see when He took my hand and led me away from Paxil is that there is a connection between beauty and pain, but it is not pathological. One need not be destroyed by pursuit of beauty. Our ability to sense pain is the backdrop against which we realize the freedom of beauty. The knowledge that beauty is a victory over pain and darkness, even as an unconscious awareness, makes the beauty fully beautiful.

I've listened to the Don McLean song and wept for Vincent, knowing that I could have loved him, too, realizing that this world was not meant for any of us, for we are all too beautiful for it. I wish he had known the comfort of the One who made beauty, comfort that could carry him through those dark times. Until recently I only thought I could understand those dark times, in a tiny way, by comparison with my own. I didn't understand the mania that drove him to paint, paint, paint in that brilliant Provençal sun, the irresistible pressure to respond to that light, to rejoice in it, to drink it in and become one with it.

> Now I think I know what you tried to say to me,
> How you suffered for your sanity, how you tried to
> set them free.
> They would not listen, they're not listening still.
> Perhaps they never will.
>
> Don McLean, 1971

At the risk of stating the obvious connection, this seems so parallel in my mind to Jesus' sufferings. Is it any wonder I worshiped in front of that painting?

To Look on His Face

"For we know in part and we prophesy in part, but when completeness comes, what is in part disappears. When I was a child, I talked like a child, I thought like a child, I reasoned like a child. When I became a man, I put the ways of childhood behind me. For now we see only a reflection as in a mirror; then we shall see face to face. Now I know in part; then I shall know fully, even as I am fully known" (I Corinthians 13:9-12).

Back to my favorite chapter of Scripture. When He first saved me, I heard the words of this chapter and desired above all to seek the greatest of all, love. I asked Him to teach me to love, not so I could possess the greatest gift, but so I could give that gift to Him. He searched me and knew me, even my most secret thoughts (Psalm 139); He did not see as the world sees, but looked on my heart (I Samuel 16:7). In His wisdom and mercy, He accepted my living sacrifice (Romans 12:1).

Tonight He called to me to walk in the Garden, again. He usually waits until sunrise, but this night there was something particular to show me. I do not mind being wakened, especially by this Friend, so I eagerly followed Him outside. Yes, outside. I know the middle of February is not amenable to basking in the middle of the night, but I donned my fuzzy pink bathrobe and stepped out onto the porch into the still strong and beautiful light of His now half moon. I breathed in the perfume of the daphne He planted here for me (by the hand of a former owner) and sat down on the front steps to gaze up at His face.

Everything is so beautiful to me now; each thing I see seems new. He does make all things new (Revelation 21:5). Looking at the moon it is as if nothing were ever so beautiful, and I realize I am looking up into His face; that is why it is so lovely. He is with me, showing me meaning and purpose and plan, and it is all for my good (Romans 8:28). He brings to mind verse after verse about His care and provision and protection, and the message keeps coming back to the idea that He has plans for me, and they are plans for good, for a hope and a future (Jeremiah 29:11).

This path I have chosen to walk is not a path I designed, nor is it a path I have walked in error. I have walked, following my Shepherd, and where I am is where He has led me. When my faith was new and I was less confident in it, when I was still learning to hear His voice, I surely made many choices that were not His best for me. He kept letting me choose, kept protecting me, kept guiding me, and used even my errors to accomplish His purposes of completing me (Philippians 1:6). And, because I do not live alone, and I am only one of His children, He used my choices and my life to accomplish His purposes in others' lives as well.

Tonight, looking up into His face, at His moon, I realized that now I know His voice, and it no longer sounds like my conscience or my rationalizing. In the same way that I have learned to distinguish between Frank Sinatra and Tony Bennett (I used to think all the singers of that era sounded alike), I can now distinguish Jesus' voice from all others, almost at the first note. I know His footfall as well as I know the sounds of each of my children and my husband moving through my house. I know the fragrance of His breath as He speaks softly to me, close to my ear, my face, my heart. I know the sounds of the Garden as He passes by.

Sitting in the moonlight, drinking in these revelations, I realized that the moon, the beautiful moon I have so rejoiced to see, is now halfway gone toward disappearing from my sky. The cycle of light and darkness cannot stop; it is part of life here in this world. I remembered that the darkest of nights, though, is the night we say there is a new moon. New hope, new promises. A future, even in the darkness.

I begged Him never to let me forget, never to let me stop seeing His face. And He showed me what He had brought me to see.

The sky tonight had a few clouds passing through it as silver shadows. Funny how, in the light of the moon, the obscuring clouds look brighter than the night sky. Our moon was not clouded, though, when He had me look up from my prayer. "Keep watching," the Voice whispered.

As I obeyed, I saw clouds moving toward the moon. I kept my eyes fixed on that brilliant half-circle. Barely breathing in the chilly air, I watched as the clouds passed between the moon and me, but the moon did not grow any dimmer. I watched carefully, wide-eyed, surprised that even though the shadows were definitely between us, the moon and its light were unchanged. For several minutes I watched, until the clouds had all passed by. The light of the moon stayed as strong and pure throughout as it had been when He first wakened me and called me outside.

This is the promise, then. If I keep my eyes on Him, there will be light to see, even in darkness. Even when the Enemy sends clouds or the world and its cares cast shadows of uncertainty, there will be light. The One who first spoke into the darkness still speaks into it today, and when He says, "Let there be light" – there is light! So simple, so reassuring, so empowering.

How He loves us – so much that He promises to give us the desires of our hearts (Psalm 37:4). Only He is able to

Deborah L.W. Roszel

work all that out for so many of us at once, but He is faithful to all His promises, and He cares for us.

Amen. Let it be so.

State of the Union

Sense. Sensitive. Sensual. Sensuous.

We put such fine degrees of distinction into our words to help us understand and communicate. To help us sense and make sense. We humans want to know and be known so obsessively, as a matter of survival, that we categorize and organize and separate and label things continually in an effort to make order of our world. At least I do. At least I did.

Now I receive information in whole packages. It's that silly-sounding word, *gestalt*. Awareness of God's work comes to me in particular situations, perfect and entire. I speak a sentence or hear a phrase or simply notice some piece of His work, and suddenly it is as if a book has been downloaded into my brain, a book with the explanation of what I've just sensed, detailed on the physical level, past, present, and sometimes future, and on the spiritual plane, which is timeless and spaceless. Download complete. Just like that.

The Lord our God, the Lord is One. And yet He is Three in One. I know it's a concept that we've struggled with as people forever. But we've overdone the struggle. At least I have. I've been trying to understand it by understanding more about each of the Three. Trying to figure out which Who does what. I guess I've never really had a concept of the One that felt as if I could communicate simply with Him. Limited, finite creature that I am, there's only the one of me and I've had enough trouble getting along with that one. I couldn't imagine a being who was three in one.

I still can't imagine it in the sense of being able to get my mind around a clear picture of God. But I can see Him now, with the eyes of my spirit. All at once, Three in One. One God, one faith, one baptism. He in me, I in Him. Unity.

This is part of the mystery of being in this Garden. Just as I sense all of God in a new way, all of the Garden is available to me all the time. Each individual part of it, but also all of it, all at once. And all of me is now open to walking with God, not just some of the individual parts. My, how much greater the whole is than the sum of those parts.

I never even imagined there could be this much wholeness. I was too busy trying to understand the parts, of which I have quite a few, trying to make sense of the many ways God was reaching to me through the tiny cracks I allowed to stay open to Him. Hiding inside my rubble fortress, I couldn't even see all of myself, much less comprehend the All of God. He spoke through my body in pain and pleasure, sickness and health, work and rest; through my mind in challenges and problem solving and teaching and learning; through my spirit in music and painting and sculpture and drama and dance. So many ways I sensed Him. So many, many deep and yet disparate experiences.

When I was expecting my first child I kept a book handy at home: Lennart Nilsson, *A Child Is Born*. It's a book of photos of pre-born children, with narrative explaining the stages of development. It's a scientific work; because of the beauty of the photography one might call it an artistic work; but it is not a religious work. (Must keep those categories clear.) It was very useful as a guide to me as I waited and wondered about this new person being put together inside of me. What part is God working on this week? Check the book and see!

What Mr. Nilsson could not convey, through no fault of his own but because a photograph and a book cannot capture it, is that the person God was building was not a combination of leg buds that grow into legs, feet and toes and toenails, plus arm buds that grow into arms, hands, etc., plus a primitive arterial swelling that develops into a heart serving arteries and veins and capillaries, plus all that other stuff he told me about in his book. My son arrived here on the outside of me as a human being, whole, perfect, complete, alive, and beautiful, SO very much more than the sum of all those fantastic photographs and the incredible narrative that helped me to imagine what was happening all along. He was more than science and art, more than my thinking and understanding could have even theorized.

"What if it's a boy?" "What if it's a girl?" "What if it's a redhead?" I never asked, "What if it's a person?" but that was the question whose answer broke my heart and left me weeping in the hallway outside the nursery window, tears running down to my toes, looking at my son and not being able to touch him. (I didn't know that first morning after his birth that I could have asked the nurse to bring him to me when I woke up. Our kind and wise pediatrician met me as I returned to the room alone and wet-faced, and at once ordered "the baby" to be brought to me.)

I use words carefully, and I always cringe a little when I hear the phrase "the miracle of birth." I think it's a misuse of the word "miracle" because, well, birth is just a natural and scientifically quantifiable process. It's part of life. I realize the odds are against it, against conception, against development, against live birth. I've read the numbers, how many pregnancies end before the mother even knows there is a pregnancy. I lost a baby of my own before I knew her name or even if she was a she or a he. For heaven's sake, the mother's body is designed to treat invading sperm as enemies, targets for chemical warfare. But still, once the process is underway, it seems that birth is just another part of it. Not a miracle. Not a divine intervention into human affairs that cannot be explained any other way.

In my compartmentalized life under the rubble, this truly was my response to that phrase, "the miracle of birth." In spite of my absolute opposition to abortion, in spite of my firm adherence to creationism, in spite of my constant work to make my faith compartment line up with my science compartment, until I typed while God dictated this morning, it never occurred to me that the miracle of birth really is a miracle. Only God could pull it off – there is no scientific way to explain the creation of a person.

I know, because there is no scientific way to explain me, as I am now, re-born in a way to this life with God, delivered from the artificial womb where I had retreated to be safe. Whole. Complete. Perfect. Created by God to live in this world, in His Garden, to know Him and to glorify Him and to enjoy Him forever.

And to take things as wholes, not as parts. My senses teach me, I am sensitive to God, I enjoy sensuality, I am sensuous. It's all one, sanctified by God, made new in Him in my rebirth, holy and acceptable in His sight. I am my Beloved's, and He is mine. We are one.

Serenity.

Cocktail Party Small Talk

"Hi, I'm Debbie. It's so good to meet you. What do you fight?"

I so hate inane conversation. I feel such a pressure to get to what a person is really about, where he finds meaning, what matters to him. "What do you do?" is such a wide-open query. We've trained ourselves to place our career descriptions in the blank following that question. But for most people, a job is not nearly all they do. It's often asked of me, but I never ask it of another without feeling false, so I usually ask it in a different way, trying to get to meaning. "How do you spend your time when you're not in choir?" "What do you do for fun?"

One of the things that has always impressed me about Jesus is His ability to speak directly to the point of need in a person's life. Sitting beside a well in Samaria, he skipped the pleasantries. (Or John didn't record them, which is possible. Like me, he may have judged them to be nonessential.) But whether He made small talk or not, He did get to the heart of the matter – with his first (recorded) sentence, although its depth unfolded over the length of the discourse.

"Give me to drink" (John 4:7). The One Who made water asks this woman, who has spent her life trying to please men in an effort to be whole, to please Him by giving Him water. Of course she can't ignore the request. Who knows how long the current relationship will last? She hasn't had a great track record so far. This guy seems different, somehow. Something in the eyes.

The story continues; you know it well. I've always taken away from it the desire to be able to see the way He sees, to know a person's need and be able to move the conversation there, to bring the Living Water to quench the other's thirst. He has poured so much into me; I am filled to overflowing. The needs are so great, the thirst so apparent, and yet we skirt the issue, making up empty phrases to hide the lack, both to seem okay to the other and to keep from looking at his emptiness ourselves.

God gave us eyes for a reason. Why do we choose not to see?

I can no longer avoid seeing. I can't close my eyes. I haven't been able to since my first overseas mission trip four years ago.

He gave us voices for a reason as well. Why do we choose not to speak, or to speak wastefully?

Now, full of joy, I can no longer avoid speaking. And my desire is never to speak wastefully. I don't wish to waste a moment of the life God has granted me. And I want more than ever – with much more urgency than I did when He called me to missions thirty-five years ago – I want to be sure all of His precious and beautiful children receive a drink from that Fountain.

And off I go.

Healing Balm

This morning my Friend woke me earlier than usual, but not to write. He woke me with a hug, a hug that held me and surrounded me, enfolding my entire body in the warmth and release of the embrace. I lay in His arms, ecstatic and at peace, feeling every part of myself touched and accepted and redeemed in His perfect love.

When I was able to think, to move beyond the sensory and emotional details of the moment, I had no words to say or to write. I waited. *This is our morning, our time,* I thought. *What would He have me do?*

I remembered a book, a book I was given just last night: *Journey to the Well: A Novel,* by Diana Wallis Taylor. My friend Estine came to visit yesterday evening, and she told me she had just finished a novel. It was about the Samaritan woman at the well. Startled by having just realized my connection with that woman the day before, I stopped her. Was she really telling me this? Of course she was. My Friend is not mine alone, and He is working all things for all of our good all the time. Estine had been moved by the book, and she had been moved not to return it to the library on her way here, and then she had been moved to tell me about it. I told her she was prophesying over me as she summarized the joy this woman felt running back to the village and sharing her news, and how others followed her eagerly back to hear this Man who had told her everything she had ever done.

This morning, then, after another reminder that I am His in all of my "parts": body, soul, mind, spirit – however I choose to divide myself, He sees me as a whole being, as His good and perfect treasure – after that warm and beautiful reminder, He had medicine for me. In the dance of the moment, I saw Him watching over me and ministering to me in the same way that I watched for so many nights recently, bringing help and healing to my husband and children. I'm still dancing that part, too, for one son who needs to wake up each night at 2:00 for help. It was natural, then, to find Him joining me, and not surprising that He brought help for me. He's been leading the dance all along, but sometimes He steps back and watches me. On this morning, His hands folded over mine, and He bade me follow Him, not to write this time, but to read.

I didn't read very long, but as I finished the second chapter, I felt the medicine's effect. He wanted to assure me once again that this Garden is exactly where He wants me to be. He knows I have old habits of holding on to rails, of grabbing for crutches, of sitting out the dance. He knows I don't need those habits any more, but He doesn't leave me to go it alone. He keeps steadying my steps, holding my hand, His eyes locking on mine, as with His hand on the small of my back He leads me effortlessly across the floor.

Rising to come downstairs to write once again my love for Him, another old habit fluttered past. *And if I'm very careful to do it right, things will be more and more wonderful.* Sigh. Breathe. I don't have to do anything right. For one thing, I can't do it all right. For another, I don't have to do anything but follow this Man, this Friend, this Partner, this Shepherd. Follow, little lamb. Know His voice, and follow.

The joy I have now does drive me to share, and I do run, and skip, and want to fly. Like the woman at the well, I am so overcome with the magnitude of what He has done for me, so filled with the power of wholeness and redemption that I am bursting to tell and bring others to see. I hope that, like her, I will soon find others flocking behind me, eager to meet this Man and find healing for themselves at Jacob's well.

How Great Thou Art

When I sing, I hear my own voice, of course, but I sometimes try to match my voice with someone else's. So my mind hears that person's pacing and tone and shaping of the notes, that person's breathing and rising and falling. Of course in choral singing I'm doing that deliberately, trying to achieve that perfect blend that contributes to the best choir performance. Even when I sing alone in an empty house, though, I sometimes fancy I'm singing along with someone.

I seem to be designed for singing along, for fellowship. It feels right – not lonely – even though I am very aware that in the existential sense I am always alone. Perhaps the desire for fellowship, for union with another, is part of what drives us to God. Certainly we were made to be with Him, not alone. So the desire for communion is not an indicator of emptiness but a reminder of fullness, and thus we are able to move beyond the limited truth of philosophies that try to explain existence, and into the infinite truth of relationship with the One Who gives us life.

Hmm. I was praying specifically for my little daughter this morning when she came to me after a bad dream, praying that she would grasp the knowledge that Jesus is always, always with her and that she would never, never be alone. She comes to me so openly with her hurts and fears; I want to give her the love and acceptance and comfort that have been given so freely to me, to build in her the confidence I lost when I was nearly her age. When I see her unmasked need for fellowship, I must help her meet that need. It is not a curiosity, just something that makes her different from her brothers. It is a gift that God can use to bring her ever closer to Him.

Yesterday we had a long visit with a young man who is the first in his family to draw near to God. This fellow has watched and has taken many notes. He has seen that families whose parents take a firm stand for Christ (as differentiated from "for church") pass on to their children not only the knowledge of the faith but the faith itself, and those children grow up to do things much greater and mightier than the parents ever did. The blessing of faith continues through the generations. This young man is trusting that when he starts his own family, his faith will be as a wall across the history of his family, breaking the generational curse of faithlessness and beginning a new history of blessing.

I look at my oldest son, who now has a vision for a new ministry adventure surpassing anything I would have dreamed at his age. His eyes are so clear, undimmed by worldly cares or hurts. How grateful I am that we were "overprotective" parents, as the occasional childish accusation goes, and that we were able to keep most of the muck of the road from hitting him in the face as he traveled along with us.

All these thoughts come together in my mind like the different voices of an orchestra. God joins so many parts of my life together to make the music that accompanies me. He's a great composer.

But back to singing. I was able to attend a music conference once with my favorite choir director of all time, Lucy Anne (Fisackerly) Adams. (I love her Scottish maiden name, so I bring it up whenever I can.) Anyway, we had a two-night, two-day conference. We received music the first night for a complicated piece, and we performed it together – for one another and for God – at the last meeting. It was the biggest group I'd ever sung with, and the experience was transcendent. Of course it helped that most of the people in the choir were choir directors with beautiful voices, but that simply gave more height to my joy as I perceived the distance between my ability and training and theirs – that I was counted worthy to be in their number.

When I get to heaven, I'll again feel unworthy and worthy at the same time. The saints who've gone before, for all the ages, the saints who are dying for Christ even as I write, will welcome me into their number joyously and allow me to join my own small voice with theirs to give my most beautiful gift alongside theirs in a supremely beautiful offering to God. Forever. Really, I don't think I'll mind even if I have to hold a choir folder for all that timeless time.

This morning I reviewed the music from Sunday morning's church service. When I got to "How Great Thou Art," I made a research side trip. I found a history of the hymn, and its history added new depth to the joy I had singing it yesterday. I felt a sense of history, of people singing this song to God for many years. Having read about the hymn, I realize my sense of its scope was barely brushing the surface.

The poem was originally Swedish, "O Store Gud." I like that, because part of my heart is tied to the Nordic countries. The poet was moved to write it after a particularly resplendent day outdoors. The addition of a folk melody turned the poem into lyrics with an element of antiquity. The hymn has been modified and translated and reworked in Swedish, Russian, German, English, and who knows how many more languages by now. It has been significantly used in mission efforts, and some of the English lyrics were specifically inspired by God's work in the mission field.

So, when I stood in the choir and sang "How Great Thou Art," Lord, You were allowing me to stand with people of many nations, many times, many tongues, singing to You and praising You for Your wondrous works. Just as You bring to me disconnected thoughts that are actually related when viewed from Your perspective, You brought together all of these voices and, outside of time, You heard them all, all at once.

Now that was some mass choir. No wonder I couldn't stop smiling.

Thank you.

Reconciliation

Continuing our musical performance, we haven't heard yet from the Communion section. Yesterday's communion at Renovation Church brought me to my knees, but not at a rail.

The pastor of this unusual church is a Louisiana-bred (read: African, Cajun, French, Cherokee) former pro football player and trained lawyer who went to seminary and moved to Atlanta without a job because God told him to plant a church here.

My kind of guy. Eclectic. Not to mention passionate.

Communion there is more in the line of liturgical churches where the communicants go to receive the sacraments rather than pass them to one another in the pews. (Or open a pre-packaged wafer and grape juice from a bucket. Gag.) At Renovation, the pastors (or celebrants or whatever they call them here) stand around the perimeter of the room, each holding a tray with a cup and a loaf. We tear the bread ourselves (very visceral, very meaningful) and dip it into the cup and then partake. It grabbed my heart the first time. His body broken for me (by me), His blood shed for the remission of my sin (and I stain the body with His blood). Almost a swoon, but not quite.

Yesterday we sat on the second row, so instead of going to an assistant on the side, we were to go forward to receive communion from Leonce, the eclectic pastor. As he began the celebration, I knew something special was coming. I could not take my eyes away, first from his face, then from his hands. Huge, powerful, beautiful, smooth, black hands, dwarfing the loaf he held. I wondered about the color of Jesus' strong hands, holding the loaf that night in the upper room, preparing to allow Himself to be broken. I wondered if His hands were large or small, rough or smooth. I knew they were beautiful.

And the next section of the orchestra joined in. I read last summer, for the first time, *Uncle Tom's Cabin*. The character of Tom so embodied the love of Christ, so inspired me anew to faithful following. The story in all its pain and ugliness and darkness still had light throughout because of Tom's unwavering faith in the One Who ultimately must triumph. And the music of that story, and of that terrible period of our nation's history, joined the song of communion.

Suddenly Leonce was not just a man – any more than I am just a woman. We were both standing in the stream of history, of His story (as the Christian curriculum providers like to say), and we were both fully aware of all that has gone before and of where God wants to take us. This is a church founded specifically for the purpose of reconciliation, of renovation in the relations between and among all races in the city. We lost power during the last service and found out yesterday that it was because a man had stolen a car in an adjoining county and, while running from police, had driven into a utility pole and knocked out power for a several-block area. "Welcome to church in the city," Leonce said with a smile. "This is why we're here."

I braced myself to walk down the steps to the Table, grateful for a rail to hold along the way. I concentrated on not letting my tears fall before the Meal. I determined to look in Leonce's face, into his eyes, after receiving the sacraments. And so I did.

I made it back to my seat as my vision blurred, and I fell to my knees in front of the folding chair, letting the tears flow freely as I thanked the Almighty, Who preserved a people who were beaten and torn and degraded and debased, and in His mercy also preserved those who brought down the whips and forged the chains that kept them there. It meant the world to me, as I told Leonce at lunch, to be able to bow and receive communion from this brother, this man whose history is so very different from mine, who is now willing to give what was withheld from his people for so long, even at the cost of receiving more of the same treatment.

Humility. Meekness. Power under control. In Christ's name and for His sake. Amen.

He Promised Me the Moon

I awoke early again today. It makes me giggle, now, when my eyes open in the darkness of my bedroom. I always know that it doesn't really matter what the clock says; it's time to get up. This morning it happened at 5:00 a.m. I am not kidding; this is serious stuff. I am rising before dawn and there are no cows to milk, there is no lengthy commute, there is no medicine to take or deliver. But I practically leap out of bed and run down the stairs to begin writing.

I can't lie there in the dark, once my eyes are opened. Yes, as I write this I see it is a metaphor for our walk with Christ in general. But in the temporal reality of my life right at this moment, I am in a darkened house, at the end of a dark night (new moon is tomorrow), and I can't go back to sleep because of the Light.

I see it as brightly and brilliantly as I saw the full moon's light two weeks ago when I lay awake for hours looking on His face. The Light of His presence is so completely filling. "You fill up my senses," John Denver sang to his beloved Annie. My Beloved fills my senses as well; the Light fills not only my eyes, but my ears, my nose, my mouth – He fills me and surrounds all of me with all of Himself.

Yes, yes, I am certain there must have been many women who thought they were going to marry Jesus. There were certainly many men who gave themselves to Him fully, following Him not only to His death but to their own. Now, two thousand years later, many of us are not tuned to Him. The cares of the world, the busy-ness of business, the constant whispers from our old Enemy, the sights and sounds and smells and tastes and feelings of a fallen world, all combine to make a very effective interference that distorts His message. But then, when He was walking among men and women in the flesh, when they could know Him physically as well as spiritually, there must have been many, many people who found themselves in love with this Man as I am now.

I don't regret being in this place and time, though. Truly it must have been wonderful to sit at His feet, to watch Him walk by, to walk behind Him. But I wonder if those who had that privilege understood as I can today that the union He desires is more than physical, though it is supremely personal and intimate. I think if I were in a crowd of thousands hanging on His every word, even with my powerful imagination, the physical reality would distract me from realizing that He had come for me and would have come for me alone. So maybe there were only a few who met His eyes and were transformed like the woman at the well. I only know that I am glad, presently and eternally glad, that I received the message He is sending.

"Come, Thou Fount of every blessing, Tune my heart to sing Thy grace . . . ." I am glad my heart is tuned in.

I am also glad that He speaks truth, and that it unfolds before me just as He promises. "Only God knows the future," a preacher told us once when teaching about prophecy and its fulfillment and how to distinguish false prophets from true. Well, a week ago God told me, and I wrote it down, that if I keep my eyes on Him, there will be light to see even in darkness. This is a quick fulfillment of that prophecy.

Even when I woke up in the dark of the moon this morning, I could see. The darkness itself seemed to hold light.

When God made the world, the first thing He said was, "Let there be light." This was before He made the stars, the sun, the moon. Before glow-in-the-dark toys or low-voltage night lights. He is light, and He created light of Himself alone. This is the light in the darkness. I can see how to get out of bed and get downstairs because He lets me see. Even my eyes and the parts of my brain that process visual messages are under His control, and He tunes them to see the Light. He is Light, and He made us to be in Light, even as we are in darkness. We are in the world but not of it. Though we walk through the valley of the shadow of death, we are children of Light.

He promised me the moon, and He delivered. He promised me Light, and once blind, now I see.

Amazing grace.

The True Freedom of Choice

I wonder how the angels feel.

We're told that a difference between angels and men is that men are given the power to choose right from wrong. I don't understand how that all works, with Satan being called a fallen angel and all. But what if angels can't choose, if all they can do is serve God?

What if I had no choice but to serve God?

Would I still feel this all-encompassing joy if I had not lived without it for so long? If I had never lived in the darkness, would I be able to understand the miracle of light? If, as a child, I had not been damaged, if my faith in goodness had not been shattered, if I had never tried to build my own world, could I fully comprehend the wonder of the world He made for me?

This is why we can rejoice in trials. This is why we can count it all joy when we fall into temptation. This is what gave our Lord strength to set His face toward Jerusalem, where He knew the greatest trial of all awaited Him. For the joy that lies beyond the trial we can be joyful, but in the trial itself we can rejoice because we DO have a choice, and because the choice of obedience is the best choice, and because we receive the prize of joy when we make that choice. We win even when it looks like we're losing, because He has won for us.

The brighter the light, the darker the shadows; when we find ourselves in the darkest of times, it is because His light is so bright. The very brightness of the light creates the illusion of darkness. The darkness itself, then, rather than blocking out the Light, actually points us to it.

"I am with you always" (Matthew 28:20). "I will never leave you nor forsake you" (Hebrews 13:5). "Neither death, nor life, nor angels, nor principalities, nor powers, nor things present, nor things to come, nor height, nor depth, nor any other creature, shall be able to separate us from the love of God, which is in Christ Jesus our Lord" (Romans 8:38-39). Not clouds on the face of the moon. Not darkness. Not fear. Not loneliness. Nothing, nothing can keep God, Who is love, from being with us once we have answered His call, and even before we have answered.

He seeks us. In the darkness, I can laugh like a child playing hide and seek, because I know that the One who is "It" will always, always find me, even if I get lost on the way back to base. I can listen for His steps even while I cower in my "safe" place, hoping not to be found and yet trembling, hopeful that He will find me and that we can run together, one after the other, hair flying in the breeze, laughing and squealing and rejoicing in the moment. In the light.

Could we appreciate the beauty of the sunrise without its contrast to the dark of night? Not fully. There is joy in seeing the light after coming through darkness. But the sunset is also beautiful, and it is the precursor of darkness. This is the other side of joy, the longing unfulfilled that can only be fulfilled by more longing, the ecstasy of loving the Beloved, of knowing and being known and wanting always to know more. Watching the sun leave the sky, I know night is coming, but it is full of the same beauty and love and joy as the day, because He is in it.

Lord, let me look at my personal darkness, when it comes, with the same longing and peace and confidence. When I am faced with temptation, give me strength to flee, but if I still fail, let my eyes not be clouded by the dirt of the ground where I fall. Let me still see Your Light in my darkness, and let me hear Your voice calling, "Allee, Allee, In-Come-Free!"

I don't know how the angels feel, but I feel glad that I can choose to answer that call.

The Voice of Correction

$\mathcal{A}$nd . . . that just happened.

Or, "And, sheeeeee's . . . SAFE!"

This morning He found me stroking my chin about an idea that was troubling me. I suppose I was actually fiddling with a stone I had picked up to examine more closely. Yes, that's exactly what it was – a worry stone. This is getting better with every step, with every letter I type. (*Thank you, Lord.*)

So I came downstairs, carrying this fairly heavy stone, turning it over in my hands. I studied its faces, for it had many. I thought I might as well start writing about it. But the words didn't come easily. They were forced, colorless, empty. After a couple of paragraphs, I stopped. No wonder. How could I type with a stone in my hands?

I didn't want to give up, but something was wrong. My feet were dragging; my head was down. I'd stopped feeling the warmth and beauty of the Garden, although I knew it was there. I was a step away from it, though; all my attention was centered on this piece of rock I was holding. And it wasn't even a pretty rock. Not even attractive in the way that rocks might be. Well, maybe to another rock . . .

But I am not a rock, even though I was starting to feel like one. "I will set no unclean thing before my eyes." This was an unclean thing, a piece of rubble left over from an explosion, thrown far through the air, half buried in the dirt. And I, curious I, had picked it up. And set it before my eyes.

Now why would I do that? Why would I pick up a piece of trash and look at that rather than stay in the rapture of my Friend's face, gazing on His beautiful Garden? Was it some sentimental weakness, some unrecognized desire to connect with a piece of my past, a fragment of the fortress of garbage I'd built around myself?

By God's grace, I realized something was wrong. I don't want these morning visits to stop, but I also don't want them to become a religion. I haven't missed a morning yet, and that appeals to my perfectionism. This relates to the stone I was carrying, which was made of philosophies and approaches to life. But that perfectionist stone, the one that I'd polished and cherished the most, from inside my castle, got pretty completely fragmented when He lifted me out of that place. Of course, that means that as I walk barefoot through the Garden, tiny grains of perfectionism still cling to my feet, and an occasional pebble is there to trip me.

When I felt the pebble underfoot this morning, I stopped. I realized I was not looking around, but only down at my oddly familiar stone. I lifted my eyes, and it took a moment to refocus; the brightness of the Garden had been momentarily shaded by my bent head. I said aloud, "I want to see Your face."

"Yes."

"Well, You promised."

"Yes." (Pause.) "Do you hear yourself?'

I was pouting!

Bowed head. Not bent away from Him, as it had been, but bowed before Him. "Yes. And I know I don't deserve it. And I'm sorry."

His fingers under my chin. My face cradled in His hand. He lifts my face, and He is smiling down at me, as beautiful as ever.

I'm pretty sure that's how conviction and repentance are supposed to work.

So that's what's new today.

Trinity Waltz

One, two, three. One, two, three. Left, right, left. Right, left, right. Press, lift, lift. Down, up, up. I've been waltzing since 4:30 this morning, with only a few brief trips to the punch bowl for a nap. Which is to say, I've been more awake than asleep, but never alone.

I love the feel of the waltz. I cannot hear a waltz played without wanting to dance; nor can I hear a military march without wanting to join in. Part of the irresistibility is the pull of history, the flow of time that draws me into the current of music that has moved people for centuries. When I hear a march, I get in line for review, or even for battle, alongside those thousands upon thousands of souls who have been called by the fife and drum. When I hear a waltz, though, I am in a shining gown with glittering jewels in a sparkling ballroom with thousands and thousands of spirits who have allowed their bodies to flow together above the glistening floor in a dance that is not only for one couple but for an entire community in space and time. It is as beautiful to the observer as it is to the participant. This is the dance of the Garden.

I imagine God the Father is watching us all, seated on His throne at one end of the ballroom. I suppose the Spirit is dancing with us, moving with and through us, around and within us. But the Son captures most of my attention, as ever. He is the one who came here with the sole purpose of helping me to understand and know God. He is my chosen and intended, and I am His beloved.

My Partner is strong, His back straight and lovely, in spite of trials that were meant to destroy Him. His hand holding mine is gentle; even though it has fought many battles and is surely capable of grasping power, now it is extended toward me, palm open, to receive the simple gift of my fellowship. His hand on my back is sure, and I can rest securely in this embrace, confident that He will lead me through the myriad of other dancers without ever a bump or a missed beat. I am conscious of being part of a living, breathing body giving itself to worship of the Almighty, but I hardly notice the crowd, because my Partner's presence is so all-fulfilling; I don't have a need or desire to look away from Him. His eyes, often locked on mine, also scan the room, noticing the other dancers, nodding in greeting, but watching all the changes in their movements so that He can keep our course steady. He is so in tune with me that He senses changes in my posture, my tension, my balance, and He gives me the needed support or nudge or pause, but He does it without a word or even a change in facial expression.

I find myself a little out of step and look down, then back up at His face. He smiles back, amused and quizzical, wordlessly asking, "What?"

"I almost missed, there."

"But you didn't."

"I was embarrassed."

"There is no need."

I am completely His, and nothing can ever change that. He has paid the bride price to assure that I will be His, forever. All He asks in return is my hand in His. And no misstep, no missed beat, no fall, no shadow can ever keep me from the encircling, upholding, empowering embrace of

His love. For as long as I let Him, He will lead me through this dance, over the holy ground of His Garden.

I could have danced all night, but I came late to the dance. It was nearly morning before I began. So now I will dance all day with Him.

True Blue

They're blue. The sweetest eyes I've ever seen are blue.

It's a line from an old love song, but I'm not talking about my most Beloved. These eyes belong to a friend, a young man who is actually my son's friend.

When I met him, the very first time I saw him, the love inside him almost knocked me off my feet. It had the same effect on my companions, who were also meeting him for the first time. Although I'm sure his handsome face and figure affected our perception, by the time we had spoken more than a few words of greeting I realized that it was the transforming Light inside him that drew us in.

The same Light that shines in the Garden shines in his eyes. His open heart and face make perfect reflectors of the true Light. That's why they're the sweetest eyes.

"Even though He slay me, yet will I trust in Him" (Job 13:15). Having recently seen the eyes of this young friend, having felt them drawing my heart to him and also to eternal Love, those words came to my mind this morning. An odd contrast: Those sweet eyes, and death?

But I let myself imagine it. What would I feel, what would I do if the owner of those eyes turned against me, rejected me, hurt me? I believe I would still be so transformed by the memory of Love in those eyes that I would continue to love him, to trust him to be good and to act righteously.

Deborah L.W. Roszel

Job's unfaltering commitment to follow God, expressed in his promise to trust Him no matter what, may have been inspired by an experience of Christ's eyes looking upon him. Perhaps that is why the verse came to mind this morning as I remembered my young friend's eyes: they reminded me of Christ's. Since I, too, have seen the eyes of Christ, since He has smiled at me and shown me the Light, I know that I never wish to look away or follow any other.

What's in a Name?

"What should we call this one?"

My children have gerbils as pets. Naming them is, for us, an important part of befriending them. It also helps us keep up with which one we're talking about, since they have a tendency to look pretty similar to one another. They come in different colors, but all the black ones look a lot alike, as do the blonde ones and tan ones and "lavender" (gray) ones.

So we study each new arrival. (Another trait of gerbils is their fertility.) Once it's old enough to have fur and open eyes, we watch how it behaves. We look for marks that distinguish it. These give us ideas for names. We've had one called "Squirt" because he was so fast at wiggling out of our hands and getting to the other side of the cage. "Lightning" was just about too fast to catch. We've had "Dipstick," whose tail ended in a contrasting color; "Moonshine," our first (shiny) black-coated one, and her daughter, "Moonbeam." They've also been named after people, especially since my daughter has been old enough to name them. She thought they were pretty, so they got to be named after pretty friends of her older brothers: Brandy, Lauren, Heather. We've also had Taylor and Swift.

Parents go through this process of naming even before knowing our children. We want to choose names that are meaningful. Sometimes we choose names to honor someone important to us. My firstborn is named for my father and a distinguished ancestor of my husband. Sometimes we name them for people in the Bible; we know many Joshuas and Lukes and Matthews, Sarahs and Rebeccas and Rachels. And sometimes we choose a name based on its meaning: Christopher – Christ-bearer; Rufus – red-headed; Jolie – pretty.

In Scripture, God is also called by many names, depending on the original language. He calls Himself "I Am." At different times He is "The Lord on High," "The Lord Our Provider," "The Lord Our Refuge." Even in our English Bibles, Jesus is called "Lord," "Christ," "Rabbi," and "Messiah." These numerous names for God are all intended to give us an idea of who He is. Each name is a piece of a puzzle, and all together they give us at least a limited understanding of this God who wants to be our friend.

What am I called? My given name, Deborah, has shortened forms. Most folks call me "Debbie;" some call me "Deb;" one friend sometimes calls me "Deborah." Some people, usually those I've taught or led in Sunday school or another church activity, call me "Miss Debbie." Each name carries with it a different feeling. The name someone chooses to call me tells me something about how that person feels about me at that moment. In addition to my children, a few of their friends choose to call me "Mom." That one is very special. It's an honor to me to be called that name, because being a mom is a call from the Lord to nurture, guide, challenge, and aid someone in becoming what God intends him to be.

Then there are pet names. "Sweetheart," "Honey," "Sugar." In general these are names that convey a love that is more than friendly. Used by the wrong person, they can be warning signs: Dangerous Person Ahead. Of all the names I am called, though, there is one that is my favorite.

Isaiah 43:1 "But now thus saith the LORD that created thee, O Jacob, and he that formed thee, O Israel, Fear not: for I have redeemed thee, I have called thee by thy name; thou art mine."

As a daughter of Israel by faith, I am also a recipient of that promise. My experience with God reflects it. He has come to me and called me by name; He has spoken to me to wipe away my fears; and He has said to me, "You are mine."

"Mine." I'm His. That's the best name of all.

Unhelpful Self-Help

I get frustrated with self-help books and sermon points that purport to give me the keys to success in some area of my life. Sometimes they're actually helpful, but often the Six Easy Steps seem as impossible to accomplish as the original goal. "How to Be a Perfect Hostess" – I have to seat guests where? In my living room, where my family also does schoolwork, plays games, changes clothes, feeds pets, folds laundry, reads books and takes naps? Oh, great, now I have to get a book on how to keep my living room clean.

I'm glad God doesn't write self-help books. He knows we're beyond self-help, because our selves are beyond help without His intervention. So, for example, He didn't tell me to keep my living room clean. He said, "Show My love and grace to these My children as they need to be guests in your home." Something along the lines of, "If you love me, feed my sheep." So, in love and obedience to Him, I tidied my living room so that His children could find comfort there. And if His children show up at the door while the living room is still full of school papers and game pieces and dirty clothes and pet food and clean laundry and books and pillows – well, I just sort of push everything aside and make a place to sit and visit while saying a silent prayer that they will not be offended or made uncomfortable by my clutter, and that my heart will listen to God and to my guests rather than to the piles of stuff calling my name and distracting me from His work.

My friend Kathy must have known this when she visited me here right after I had moved to this place big enough to accommodate guests. (*Now* I know that *any* place is big enough to accommodate guests, but I didn't know it then.) She had always been a hostess for parties and Bible studies and showers and dinners; I had always wanted to minister in that way but couldn't figure out how to work it out with three small children in a small house. I don't even know if I had ever shared that desire with Kathy. I know I never expected to live in a house the size of hers, but this new one was a step in that direction. Regardless of what she knew, she spoke words from God to me when she visited me the first time, and they never left me: "Use it well."

The desire of my heart this morning is to be able to speak words like that to those around me. My life now is so full, so overflowing with joy, love, hope, peace. I want everyone to have access to this; I know it is God's desire as well. But I know from history what Jesus foretold, that even the sign of Jonah would be insufficient to get the attention of some people in the world around me.

And it will be pointless to give them self-help steps. Dance naked in the Garden? No, that won't do. Sit outside in the middle of the night and gaze at the moon? I wasn't really gazing at the moon, though, I was looking into His face. How can I tell someone to look into Jesus' face, when they can't even see Jesus? I don't want to be just another useless book gathering dust on the shelves of discouraged, downtrodden, desperate souls seeking salvation. (Now THAT sounds like a Baptist sermon.)

Perhaps I could develop a list of points on how to know you're hearing from God.

Everything you see or hear or feel or smell or taste will remind you of God and His love and plan for you. Every interaction with another human being, whether casual or intentional or even supremely intimate, will remind you of God and His love and plan for you. You'll catch yourself smiling at green beans. (That really happened to me. I was so full of joy just walking through the grocery store that I couldn't stop smiling, even at canned green beans.)

I really don't think this is going to work.

Dear Lord,

You are mystery beyond all solving, truth beyond all explanation. Thank you for revealing Yourself to me. Please guide my steps so that I will ever be in the place where You want Your message delivered. Please grant that I may be able to communicate to others the message You would have them hear. Please touch their ears and their hearts so that they will be able to receive Your words. I surely can't figure it all out, but I know You can make it happen. I believe You want to make it happen and that You want to use me in that effort. I will myself to obey, as much as it is in my power to do so, and ask You to use my best efforts – and my worst – to accomplish Your purposes through me.

Love, Me.

It sounds crazy, but it just might work.

All I Want to Do Is Dance

I could sing of Your love forever.
I could sing of Your love forever.
I could sing of Your love forever.
I could sing of Your love forever.

Martin Smith, © 1994
Curious? Music UK

This was the chorus in my head when my eyes opened today. The call came from the wind chimes on the front porch, so I guess the wind is singing His praises this morning.

I still haven't heard a rock cry out. That's something else to look forward to.

The raindrops dance before the Lord, and so do I. The trees are swaying in time, arms uplifted. I love it when the music moves me so much that my arms are raised. They raise themselves, it seems, and my hands stretch upward, aching to touch His face. I would say that the trees stand a better chance of touching Him than I do, but that would not be so. For as I stretch toward heaven, my Friend is leaning down toward me, His face so close that I can touch it with my outstretched fingers. I expect He does that for all His worshipers, but I don't usually open my eyes to look around and see. I know He can, though.

Hmm. Sometime I should ask a man what his feelings are in such a moment. Mine are so intense, the outstretched

Deborah L.W. Roszel

hands, the aching to touch and be touched, they would be classified as sexual by a scientific observer whose theories don't allow for God. I am indeed in love with this Friend, and I do indeed desire Him passionately. I am His bride and He is my Head. The all-consuming nature of such a moment is, in a technical sense, orgasmic. But I am female in this human body, and I wonder how the physical experience of worship differs for a male.

What did David say? He was a pretty hardcore worshiper, I think. He danced naked in the street, in the middle of the day, that one time. I've not been transported to that level yet. Let's see . . . Psalm 42: "As the deer pants for streams of water, so my soul pants for you, O God." Psalm 47: "God has ascended amid shouts of joy, the Lord amid the sounding of the trumpets." Psalm 61: "Hear my cry, O God; listen to my prayer. From the ends of the earth I call to you, I call as my heart grows faint; lead me to the rock that is higher than I." Psalm 63: "O God, you are my God, earnestly I seek you; my soul thirsts for you, my body longs for you, in a dry and weary land where there is no water."

I think David and I share similar worship experiences. How wonderful to be allowed to serve a God Who transcends not only space and time, Who moves not only through all the physical and the spiritual, but Who even gets to us in our most intimate and personal selves in that "mysterious distance between a man and a woman." (That's not Scripture, it's U2, from the song "A Man and a Woman." God also crosses the divide between the sacred and the secular. He seems to take pleasure in messing up our tidy categories.)

So today I will dance like no one is watching. Not with any particular form or pattern, maybe. Not in a structured or classifiable way. Most likely not naked or in the street. But I will dance, because Someone is watching, and I dance for Him.

Hand in Hand

His hands are beautiful still.

I first saw them when they were outstretched, welcoming children to come to Him. His adult friends stood nearby, some scowling, some looking confused. He had just told them to let these children come. "Children? Really? Aren't they supposed to be seen and not heard or something? They don't even really count as people yet, and some of them never will; only the men are numbered when we tell who comes to these meetings."

But the Master bade them come, and come they did. And He touched them and blessed them. Surely some of them were forever changed by their experience with His hands.

He wasn't afraid to get His hands messy. Once when He healed a blind man, He spit on the ground, stirred the wet dirt with His fingers, scooped up the mud and spread it over the man's eyes. Experience with dirt, especially third-world dirt – and this was ancient third-world dirt – tells us it was nasty stuff He mixed up, at least from a health inspector's point of view. But He didn't hesitate. The hands that formed man from the dust of the ground, the hands that even made that very dust, now scooped up more of it to re-form a man.

Isn't that just like Him? He reaches down into the dirt around us, pours Himself into our world, and comes up with healing in His hands to apply to all of our hurts. He uses

71

the dirt – our mistakes, our rejection of Him, our failures of omission and commission, our sin. What else can He use? We have nothing, nothing to bring to Him to make us more acceptable, more deserving of His touch.

Lord, let our sight and our minds be focused on Your face so that when You redeem our filthy rags and make us clean, we won't get hung up on how dirty Your hands are. It's our dirt, our waste, but we are ashamed to see it, especially in the light of Your glory.

Forgive our arrogance, our pride that causes us to cover ourselves in dirt for protection while we judge those around us for looking dirty.

Redeem our hands, too, Lord, that they may touch as You touch. Let us not be afraid to reach down into the dirt of our own lives or of the lives of others. Make us willing to allow You to pour Yourself through the vessels we desire to be, to make the healing balm that You command us to bring to the sick and dying all around us.

Oh, Lord, give us tender hearts: tender but strong; sensitive and sure; discerning and loving.

And Lord, make our hands like Yours. As we stretch our hands toward You, beseeching You to be merciful and allow us to serve You, please hold our filthy hands in Yours, make them clean, and help us to stand and to walk with You and for You into the world You have made, a world we have corrupted by our own choices.

The depth of our unworthiness surpasses description. Thank you for Your forgiveness, and thank you for Your hands that touch us in spite of all. We want to do better, to make better choices. Thank you for giving us that chance.

Thank you for Your beautiful hands that extend toward us in welcome, that reach into our pain in healing, and that stretched out on a cross in love so that we could have beautiful hands, too.

Amen.

There is so much more to say about His hands, but for today I must stop. And His hands will lead me back to this place in His time.

Jesus in Blue Jeans

This morning He waved to me from a field.

I am following the interstate westward through Arkansas on the way to see my son in Oklahoma. I've driven this route before, three times in each direction. I've driven past these fields in different lights. Arkansas has seemed before like the part of the trip I have to get through to get to my goal, to be with my son at his college. The "scenery" has not even earned that name – dull, drab, flat, featureless land, with nothing natural or man-made worthy of note.

Guess what? Now that I'm riding with a new Tour Guide (as well as the fact that my husband is along for the first time and driving on this stretch), I'm seeing the scenery in a whole new morning Light.

This land is not flat or boring or featureless. I first realized it while looking at an empty field. The earth had been smoothed, but there was nothing growing there. But was it a useless void? No. As the field passed before my view, I noticed wide serpentine bands of darker soil or debris. This is the flood plain of the Mississippi, and the river regularly pours its life onto these fields. As they drink, the fields get mud moustaches, rows of them, curving along slight rises and dips in the land.

That's where He was, standing among those waves, waving. Blue jeans, flannel shirt, dirty hands. I pressed my hand to the window glass and smiled back at Him.

"I made this," He called. "Isn't it beautiful?"

And I saw that it was. Yes, this flat, muddy field was as beautiful as I am, as beautiful as the half-moon I shared smiles with during the night portion of our journey. For the same Hand had fashioned this land, the same Mind had worked out its design, the same Heart had watched lovingly over it all.

He makes all things beautiful.

Even Arkansas.

So now, on my way to see my son, I am rejoicing along with God's Son, and rather than just getting through Arkansas, I am enjoying the scenery.

(He did look cute, and a little goofy, standing out in that field, waving. I wonder if He was growing green beans there?)

Lord, thank you for the reminders. I loved seeing Your mighty river this morning, a reminder of Your all-covering provision and power as I saw the places where it had overflowed its banks to destroy and bring life to the land. I loved seeing those mud moustaches, then seeing the design copied in other larger fields whose stewards were diligently trying to preserve the soil, the nutrients, the life You give to the land. I loved noticing the many gentle swells in what I used to think was boring land, thinking about how Your eyes would never miss even the tiniest detail of that sort. Like a young mother-to-be noticing every change as life begins to swell within her, celebrating when her waistbands become too tight to contain her joy, You rejoice over every rise, every curve, every sign of life in Your creation. I love being part of that creation. Thank you for allowing me to join in Your celebration. Let me never think, "Boring," about any of Your creation, ever again. Amen.

The Truth Has Made Me Free

I am surprised, again and again, by the many ways that knowing the truth sets me free.

I know the truth, now, that the Voice I hear or sense in my heart or mind cannot be easily explained within the limitations of my American English, twenty-first-century human vocabulary. I am so far from the place Adam held as God's friend; I have lost not only proximity and fellowship but even the language to describe them.

I know the truth that it doesn't matter whether I have words to describe this. If He wishes me to share part of our experience, He will use my finite abilities to convey His infinite message, working a miracle also in the hearing of those who need to hear, just as He did at Pentecost. This frees me from the burdensome pressure of communicating to others the joy I have found, the healing and strength I have received. That pressure worked against my speaking, because instead of empowering me, it choked me, closing off the flow of my words, spoken or written. I still have the desire to share, but there is no guilt or condemnation or fear of damnation associated with my reasons to share or not to share. The sharing happens every morning as I awake joyfully to His call to listen and to write; it happens every day when He takes me to my place of need and gives me the words of blessing to help me and other members of His much-loved family. I am free to speak or to refrain from speaking, in obedience to His leading, because I know the truth: He speaks to me.

Applying truth to myself in accepting my emotions has been freeing in a different way. Previously, I have attempted to run my life based on truth *as I understood it rationally.* Emotions, as the saying goes, make up the caboose on the train, and the caboose cannot take the lead. The engine of my decision-making must be my head, which must be filled with truth. This analogy is acceptable, but I took it too seriously – a common error of my nature. Since the caboose was not supposed to lead, but only to follow after the fact, I deemed it to be inferior and unnecessary; I strove continually to behave without emotion, with perfect and serene reason in all my dealings with mankind and myself. Not surprisingly, by cutting off such a big chunk of the person God made me to be, I found it difficult to achieve the perfect success I desired. I am nothing if not committed, however, and I absolutely believed my position was good and godly, so I continued to hold on to these ideals even as the challenges of life mounted. I kept climbing over the piles of almost-successes, and quite a few real successes, and kept hoping to improve my percentages. Competitive even with myself, I would not quit.

A side effect of determining that emotions were unnecessary was this: When I could not deny an emotional response to something, I had to analyze it before acting on it. Satan loves analysis. Every feeling I experienced became so surrounded with "should" and "should not" and "what if" and "why" that I could not even honestly say how I felt about anything. Still, since I was sure I was right in ruling by reason, I persisted in the analysis and grew further and further from my own self in the process. In addition, each feeling became surrounded by fears of failure, of offense, of loss, of shame, of guilt, of condemnation – every feeling became a huge and ugly and fearful thing. Even simple pleasures became trials for me.

I know the truth, now, that emotions are a gift from God; I finally believe that to my core and am able to accept it as truth not only for others but also for myself. The surprise is that when I simply state, "I like this," it becomes just that, a simple statement of what I like. This sounds so obvious, reading it here, but it was the opposite of what I expected after such a long history of complicating my emotional life. I expected to say what I liked and then to have to defend it or explain it or excuse it in some way. In my adaptation of the train analogy, my emotions were so unimportant that they didn't deserve a mention, so it followed that mentioning them would require justification. Finally, finally, after years of my friends asking, my husband asking, my children asking, "What would you like?" I can answer and let that be the end of it. I am free because I know the truth – He has made me as a feeling person, not only a thinking person, and He loves and accepts all of me in both ways. I have been justified in Christ, and I can like things and say so.

How simple. How free.

The Lost List

In a recent visit with a friend, I spent all the time talking about myself. I wanted to ask about her time at church that evening but kept trailing off on my own stories instead, and I never got around to asking. My "old" self would have been grieved at that realization and would have said here, "I am sorry." I would have called myself selfish and thoughtless, and asked forgiveness, and I would have written another line in my list of "shoulds" – I should ask a friend first about her day, before telling her about mine. It's quite an extensive list.

But I can't find it anymore. Not sure where I laid it down. Must have dropped it here in the Garden. No, wait, I know – I was looking over it when Jesus reached into that pile of rubble I called home. That's it – I had to use both hands to hold both of His; it took both of us to get me out of there. So I laid it down, stood up, and left it behind.

Funny, I hadn't even noticed it was gone. But it makes sense that a new creature wouldn't have all the memories of the old one. Even something as prevalent in that old life as my list, in keeping with His promise, has passed away. All things have become new.

I used to read over that list continually to make sure I didn't miss anything. I was quite the Pharisee. I had taken God's law to heart, studied His grace and accepted His salvation, and then assiduously set about to interpret and apply His precepts to every detail of my life. And I had followed my own interpretations so carefully that in my mind they became His intentions, His instructions. I had grown arrogant and prideful and judgmental and hateful. Living inside my tomb of self-preservation, I presumed to be the final authority on God's message to mankind. Some even saw me that way and looked to me as an example, a model of Christian living. I was a white-washed sepulchre indeed, definitely part of that brood of vipers Christ so detested.

Yet, in spite of all that, He loved me and brought me out of it all. Praise be to God.

The Light Shone in the Darkness

*A*gain I walk with my Friend in the Garden, in the light of the full moon. The joy is still with us, but He is more earnest tonight. Again He wants to reassure me, to urge me to remember the light. He reminds me of words He has spoken before.

"The light shines in the darkness, and the darkness has not overcome it" (John 1:5).

This moonlight will always be here. At different times and in different seasons it will appear to be more or less bright, but the darkness has not and will not overcome it.

As I pass through dark times, His light will always be available to me. He wants me to remember, remember and never forget it. Keep it present in my mind, in the front of my mind, not stored away in the back.

The darkness cannot extinguish the light. His promises are sure, and He has plans for me that are good.

It seems I have some darkness ahead of me, in earthly terms. I don't know what it is, but He wants me to be ready and to know that there will always be light and that the darkness cannot overcome it. It is important for me to remember this.

"For no matter how many promises God has made, they are 'Yes' in Christ. And so through him the 'Amen' is spoken by us to the glory of God. Now it is God who makes both us and you stand firm in Christ. He anointed us, set his seal of ownership on us, and put his Spirit in our hearts as a deposit, guaranteeing what is to come" (2 Corinthians 1:20-22).

To help me keep my eyes on Him, then, I will choose to think on "whatsoever things are true, whatsoever things are honest, whatsoever things are just, whatsoever things are pure, whatsoever things are lovely, whatsoever things are of good report; if there be any virtue, and if there be any praise, [I will] think on these things" (Philippians 4:8).

I will choose not to take guilt that is not mine, not to dwell on mistakes that I cannot correct, not to accept fear that is unfounded.

I will serve in the place He has appointed for me, and I will "lay aside every weight, and the sin which doth so easily beset [me], and . . . run with patience the race that is set before [me]" (Hebrews 12:1). I will remember my reflections during my recent 10K walk about pacing myself and following the course and finishing, and I will "press toward the mark for the prize of the high calling of God in Christ Jesus" (Philippians 3:14).

So help me, God, for Your glory, I will.

Outside of Space and Time

I stepped outside by the front door very early this morning to greet the moon. The sky was full of light, but I could not see its Source. Perhaps on the back porch? I walked through the house to check, but the view was the same there. My cautious neighbors leave the security light shining all night, shining into the space between our houses, but the sky – unaffected by such a small glow – still seemed bright in spite of a solid grey covering.

I'm wondering, now that I've had my moment in the night, if He woke me to take care of someone. Everyone here seems fine, so after brief prayers for those nearby, I'll pray for my sons far away. One is likely getting up now to do some military lining up or shining up of some sort before breakfast; the other gets up in less than half an hour to start practicing his Olympic sport before daybreak.

I like knowing that God stands outside of time and watches over all of us. Now that I have a son living in a different time zone, my mind moves in sync with two clocks all the time. It's a skill learned from mothering; my attention is always divided among all my children. The division in space has come to seem quite ordinary to me, and now I am learning about the division in time as well. Imagine how God's mind moves – through all of creation, in all the time zones and all the periods of history, simultaneously attending to all the possible yesterdays, todays, and tomorrows.

I want to be more like Him. It's true, I do set the standards high.

The Burning Bush

"Now Moses was tending the flock, and he led the flock to the far side of the wilderness and came to the mountain of God. There the angel of the Lord appeared to him in flames of fire from within a bush. Moses saw that though the bush was on fire it did not burn up. So Moses thought, 'I will go over and see this strange sight—why the bush does not burn up.'"

[Why is that bush on fire in the first place? It's a calm morning. And how can it keep burning, burning, burning without changing at all?]

"'Moses, Moses!'"

[Who could that be?]

"'Here I am.'

"'Do not come any closer. Take off your sandals, for the place where you are standing is holy ground. I am the God of your father, the God of Abraham, the God of Isaac and the God of Jacob.'

"At this, Moses hid his face, because he was afraid to look at God" (from Exodus 3:1-6).

I do not think of myself as a bold person, but I am bolder now than Moses was in that moment. I see that burning bush and hear that voice. I know the voice; He does not need to remind me Who is speaking. He is the God of my forefathers as well, but He is also my God.

His message to me is different from the message He gave to Moses. Of course, it would be so. I am not Moses, and when I stand before Him in judgment, He will not say to me, "Why were you not Moses?"

He will say, "Why were you not Debbie?"

He will say that, because I was not always bolder than Moses. I was for many years more timid than Debbie.

I saw the bush – was drawn to its mystery – when I was still a child standing on the edge of budding womanhood. I knew the Voice, and knew it was trustworthy. I took off my shoes; I fell to my knees; I hid my face.

And in the darkness I placed before my face, I forgot about the Presence of the bush. The Voice was muffled by my covering, and I grew unsure of its trustworthiness.

I stood and walked away in a bit of a daze. I knew others had heard the Voice, were still hearing and following it. I thought I had heard it, but I could have been wrong. Looking at the stories in the Book, I saw tales of wonder and amazement, feats of impossibility done in the name of that Voice. *Surely, if I had truly heard the Voice, I would be doing something amazing and wonderful by now? Surely I could speak and water would pour forth from the rock.*

Ah, but Moses had heard the Voice before, too. He had been called to save His people as a young man. He acted in a rash manner and was pursued by fear, fleeing far away. He married. He started a family. He acquired responsibilities. And in God's infinite mercy, in His timeless patience, in His eternal love for His people, God called Moses again. That second time, after Moses had gained much knowledge, wisdom, and experience, he was ready to be used by God to answer the call from his youth. It would seem that Moses only thought He was running from the call, from God, when really he was simply hurrying to school so he wouldn't be late. So much to do, so little time. Forty years for Moses, but no time at all for God.

And so He has called me. And since I stand on this side of the New Covenant, the veil has been parted and I am bold to enter the Holy of Holies, to step even into the Flame and find myself burning but not consumed. And His Voice is now part of me, within me, to speak to others. The knowledge and wisdom and experience I have gained in the intervening years, He will now use to do the work He called me to, then and now.

> *Thank you, Lord, for the Flame of Your Spirit that bids me not only to listen but to come to You. If I should ever come away from here, may I shine as gold, with all my dross burned away in this crucible of Love and Joy and Power. As I walk in the Light, let it be the true Light of the World that I follow. Even in my time of darkness, Lord, I did seek to listen to Your servant Isaiah, and I trusted in You, stayed upon You, as he instructed. Let me never kindle my own fire or surround myself with my own sparks. I trust in You and You alone, seeking Your Light as I walk toward my eternal home with You.*

(And He led me to read Scripture: John 8:12; Isaiah 50:10-11; Revelation 21:23-24.)

Unstructured

I just heard the first whisper of a revelation that is going to make me want to shout.

I, contrary to what I've been telling myself forever but absolutely in line with the evidence of my life, am NOT a structured person.

Not orderly.

Not sequential.

Not linear.

I've always thought that I was "supposed" to be ordered, that it was pleasing to God for me to be so. "Evening, and morning, and at noon, will I pray" (Psalm 55:17 KJV) – it implied order and structure to me.

My Friend says otherwise. "That does not require order; it requires constancy. And you are constant."

Yes. Yes, I am constant. I have indeed been constantly seeking to follow the God I loved but did not understand. As part of that, I tried many times to develop a habit of rising early to meet Him before beginning my day. It seemed that this was the most appropriate way of meeting with God, sort of giving Him my first fruits rather than my leftovers. Eventually I admitted to myself that this was simply not workable, because I did not think clearly before ten in the morning, so no matter how "first" those fruits were, I was not giving God my best by trying to get up early. I realized that I could give Him time when I was awake and alert, and and that He would accept my offering even it didn't come to Him early in the morning.

But even as I acknowledged not being a morning person, I felt guilty because I was "supposed" to rise early to meet with my Beloved Friend. Many teachers and devotional guides supported this idea. I allowed myself to sleep in, since I often worked until well after midnight and often woke to work during the night, and I thanked God for giving me rest. But I began every day ashamed.

I developed habits to make up for my unforgivable lack of devotion. I kept a Bible by my bed and forced myself to read it first at night no matter how late I came to bed, to spend time in His Word, to please Him (because I loved Him) and to meet the expectations I thought He had of me (because I feared Him).

Even when I wanted to read a novel or needed to read for school, I feared falling asleep reading, so I read the Word first. I didn't mind falling asleep reading, per se, just falling asleep on a long day filled with busy-ness but with "no time spent with God." My strongest motivator was fear, but devotion was definitely there as well.

I knew He was with me, guiding my steps, informing my judgment, in every detail of the day. So the idea of "no time spent with God" was utter nonsense. But from within my self-constructed temple, the fortress I had built to protect myself and to please Him, somehow it seemed I HAD to do that one thing – r-e-a-d t-h-e B-i-b-l-e – or it was impossible to be right before Him. Such a demanding false religion I created! I would be a merciless God.

My God, however, is my Friend, and He is not merciless. He has shown me this very morning that I am not a structured person. He has reminded me that He made me, and the way He made me is very good. The reason I could not get up early every morning or even read my Bible every night is that I am not a regular, structured, orderly person. My house is not orderly. My routines are not regular. My days are not structured. Yet, He has walked with me through years of faithful devotion to Him. He has been with me in the midst of my messes, and He has helped me to keep my eyes on what is important. And structure, it turns out, is not all that important to God.

What a lot of life I poured out wastefully in my vain attempts to please Him. I made list after list, schedule after schedule, to try to enforce order on myself, to be more productive and therefore more pleasing to my Lord. In vain did I try to keep these standards; in vain did I grieve over my failures. Over and over, on and on, I tried and tried to be better, to do better. Yes, indeed I am constant.

My Friend watched over me all the time. He smiled indulgently as I constructed sand castle after sand castle and as the waves of my own nature and His own plan washed them away. I guess I never looked up from my busy, busy building to see Him there. I saw His feet in the sand beside me, but I didn't look into His eyes.

He has done it before, lifted me from a downcast position. This morning, as before, His hand reached down, His fingers slid under my chin, and He lifted my face to face His. This time, rather than simply bidding me look at His love, He bade me look at myself.

For the first time, I saw. All my well-intentioned attempts were unnecessary and ineffective and harmful. All my sand castles, while lovely and acceptable as sand castles, were just – piles of dirt. He liked watching me build them, because He loves me and adores me. Just as I love watching my children play, He loved watching me, but it grieved Him to let me stay there playing for so long when He had work for me to do. He had given me constancy and determination and patience and perseverance and hope and faith and strength and vision, and I was using all these powerful tools to dig in sand.

My unstructuredness, He reminds me, has allowed me to be supremely, almost infinitely flexible, which may be the most important trait for a mother of five children. My constancy has allowed me to stay on course for all these many years; all the many, many hours of work; all the many, many, many moments of challenge and uncertainty and concurrent conviction. He did not need me to be structured, and He does not now. His hand formed me, and He needed no assistance in shaping me into what I am today; my building skills, obviously so very advanced as to build castles that lasted for whole minutes before crumbling, were not needed for His construction project.

He needed me to be who He made me to be, nothing more and nothing less. By trying to be more, I had become less. Now I have seen, and I understand.

Lord Jesus, Master Carpenter and Builder of Men, thank you for taking me onto Your crew. Please forgive me for using all Your tools for the wrong purposes. Thank you for seeing my heart – seeing as You see, not as men see – and for Your gentleness in bringing me up from my knees in the sand to stand beside You. Thank you for all the building You have done in my life and in my family in spite of me, and for letting me help as I could, when I could be properly intentional, so that I know some of the results are because of me. Your pay scale is most generous; I haven't even been using the tools right, and You have still blessed me and blessed others through me. I am grateful. As You continue to show me how to use these tools, and as You give me chances to see the plans You have for me and for this world You are building, I look forward to learning and working and celebrating with You. Let's go build something, Lord!

Amen.

Staying Behind

I've been to a lot of airports. But I haven't flown much.

I go there every few weeks when my son comes home from the United States Military Academy. He is in college and in the Army, in training to rule the world. They have very high standards up there at West Point. I have very high standards, too, and I have sent them one of my best. So I pick him up and drop him off at airports.

But I stay behind.

I have loved this boy always, even since before we met. I knew I wanted him, and as soon as I saw him I was in love. I gave him the best of me, all of me, for eighteen years. He still has access to all of me, but he does not need it all anymore. I nurtured and watched him become; alongside him, and sometimes for him, I saw the vision of the bright and shining place where he is going. I drove him to the gates of the place where we would part, where he would step into that future that does not include me except as an observer. My car took him away from me, and I helped.

And I stayed behind.

Now I go to airports to see him. Airplanes bring him to me, and I rejoice, and my heart is full, and my spirit soars. Much too soon, I see him again at the airport, and the airplanes take him away. I drive him there, in my car. With a hug and a smile I release him again, back into that light that he was made for, the place prepared for him.

Deborah L.W. Roszel

And I stay behind.

Airports, they say, even I say, are happy places. They are alive with much bustle and busyness, so much excitement. Journeys are exciting, and half the people here are departing for a journey, some of them for journeys that will change their lives. I was one of those when I went on my missions trip. The other half are people coming home, which is a beautiful place to be going. Well, I guess it's not really half and half, because some of us are here to say "Farewell" or "Welcome back." The partings and reunions are part of the joy of the place, though.

It is a joy mixed with sadness. Isn't it always? The longing to be together mixed with the pain of parting, and this is the place where those two touch. But the reunions, oh, the reconnecting, the touching, the holding and beholding – the joy is inescapable. In books about cheap dates, authors suggest couples go to an airport for a few hours. All the hugging and kissing at airports is socially acceptable, so the couple can pretend to be reuniting, over and over, as long as they like, without getting in trouble. It's a silly, romantic date, a chance to be real and open with their love, to celebrate togetherness even in public.

I haven't been on one of those dates. I have, however, rejoiced in seeing others reunite. And I rejoice with them on half of my airport trips, the ones when I'm picking someone up. I rejoice with them some, even when my eyes are shaded to watch my much-loved son stepping back into the light, away from me.

But then I stay behind.

Too many airports, it seems, this morning. Too many times I have released a loved one into his light, his light that does not shine on me. Too many times I have been left standing, wondering, not knowing, building a faith without facts, making a life out of leftovers, while someone flies away.

Lord, will I ever fly? I thought I was made for it, too. I thought You told me so. I think, perhaps, I didn't pay enough attention to the flying lessons You must have given me. Or am I just not understanding?

I don't want to fly alone, though. Must I? I thought — more than that — I really did believe that I was going to fly with a companion, one You made just for me. But my companions, they — they do not want to fly. The ones who do, You send away, to fly without me.

"Lord, I am willing

to receive what You give,

lack what You withhold,

and relinquish what You take."

It says that on a piece of paper, where I wrote it down to remember it. Help me to live it, Lord. It is the desire of my heart.

Even when I stay behind.

Amen.

Missing You

"Did you miss me?" He asks.

He grins at me, a twinkle in His eye, knowing the answer.

Did I . . . Yes? No. No, yes, yes, I think I did. No?

How could I have missed Him? He has been with me always, watching my steps, encouraging, leading – sometimes carrying me. Miss Him? I don't think so. I think He's been here all along, so how could I have . . .

But there were times, yes, there were times when I could not see Him. There were times when I felt very alone. And empty. And afraid. When I forgot He was there. When I did not believe He loved me. When I thought perhaps He no longer would choose me. I missed Him then.

Huh. I guess I missed Him at other times as well. Sometimes when I was brave, not scared, and so I was taking on the world. Sometimes I missed Him then. I forgot that I didn't have to do everything on my own, and I got so busy and burdened that I shut Him out. I didn't mean to. I thought I was doing things He would approve. Perhaps I was doing them to hide from my need. Yes, I missed Him then.

He was with me in the painful times. Times of loss. Times of not understanding. Times of obedience for love, not for joy. He was with me, but I missed Him then as well.

I wanted to be closer, to know Him more, to be more like Him. I wanted His serenity, His confidence, His strength. I did miss Him.

Have I had such a sad life? No. I can answer that one with certainty. I have lived not only the life I chose, but a life that has been better than I could have hoped. I have had blessings beyond my imagination, and I continue to receive more. I have followed my heart. I have seen my dreams come true. I have known joy in the highest form I can imagine. I have felt my heart break, and fill, and break again for sheer happiness. I have seen my hopes fulfilled, my fears relieved, my prayers answered, my plans approved. Approved – yes, that was important to me, to win His approval. And I have. I have even come to understand that I never had to win it, that He gave it out of love. I missed Him a lot until I understood that.

So I missed Him in another way. Not only did I long for His presence, but I failed to notice it when it was there. He has always been with me, but I missed Him. He has been there to lead me, but I passed on by. He has waited to comfort me, but I did not look up. He has offered to raise me to my feet, but I crawled along alone.

Thank God He didn't leave. Thank God He didn't give up. Thank God He is still here, after all I've failed to do.

When I get to heaven and look into His eyes, His real eyes in His real body that has been made new, He'll welcome me home. And He just might ask, "Did you miss me?"

Yes. Yes, Lord, I did.

In the Forest,
in the Garden

What does it mean if I can't see the forest for the trees? It means I'm so focused on the details that I can't see the big picture. It means that I'm distracted from the meaning of life because I'm looking at the temporary events of life.

It happened this week. Several unrelated situations caught my attention at separate times. They were not my responsibility; I could not resolve any of them. Since each situation deeply affected someone I love, though, I got serious about praying. Each situation, each struggle, touched the very identity of the person involved, so I was really focusing on praying, a lot. And I grew somber.

What about joy? What about light?

The music is harder to hear in among all these trees. I'm not sure of the rhythm of the dance here, with sounds echoing and getting lost all at the same time. The light is different, too, as it filters through the leaves overhead. Dappled patterns of light and shadow beneath my feet make my footing seem less sure, the ground less stable. I have slowed to a walk, no longer dancing. And now the shadows have begun to speak. Their voices are familiar but not friendly; the tones are soothing, beguiling, numbing. Then, all at once, the prayers and promises, spoken before, are answered and fulfilled. I realize I'm about to step away from the path. His voice breaks through, clear and strong.

"These trees are not barriers. This forest is not a prison. *You are free.* This is a beautiful place. I am busy here, just as I am in the open spaces. This is my forest, part of my plan.

"Remember the light."

Now I understand more. If I remember the light, then I can see even when my loved ones cannot. My sight can help them not to falter. If I remember the light, then God can show me things to share with them, to encourage them in their struggles. If I remember the light, then I can fulfill my mission for His glory, and so can they.

So this is my assigned task. This is my duty: Remember the light.

Oh, God, thank you.

Fullness of Joy

*P*rior to January, I had a kind of joy. It was real, but it was not complete. It was a joy based in the certainty of the promises of God, in my confidence that I was obeying Him, in the expectation of reward for faithfulness – a joy in spite of circumstances and also because of circumstances. By "circumstances," I mean things that I did and experienced. It was also a joy in the knowledge of God and His love and care for us, His provision, His faithfulness, His constancy. Still, I was unaware of the depth and height and breadth of the joy He wanted to give me. I sensed it, even relied on it, but could not comprehend it fully.

Now – in the time since January, but also now, right in this moment – I have fullness of joy in a way that I could not have imagined then. What I sensed and relied on is so much greater than my mind and imagination could have conceived. The truth is, I had restricted my imagination so much by my burdensome legalistic religiosity that I no longer even tried to imagine how things might be. So when God would reveal something to me – something from some future time – I simply took it as true but had no idea how it would happen; I left all the details up to Him, which is fine, but I didn't even look at the beauty, the possibilities, the import of what He had shown me. He had handed me a carefully wrapped gift, telling me in the briefest terms what was inside, and I, like the mermaid Madison in "Splash," had simply said, "Pretty" - and held the gift, admiring it without opening it.

It didn't anger Him for me to do that. That in itself is a new realization for me; my false religion had much to do with anger and punishment. God, however, is not about that. He let me hold the gift as long as I wanted, because it was, in the deepest possible sense, truly a gift. Intended for me, for my pleasure and good, for me to use or not use, enjoy or not enjoy, at my will. He made me free, able to choose, and He gave me all of good creation to live in; and in accordance with His nature, He allowed me to stay in my one tiny corner until I was ready to step out.

I am so glad He helped me to step out and see His world. So much forgiveness, so much love, so much beauty, so much power, so much JOY! And now that I'm here, He is so much more real to me, and His promises are so much more immediate and accessible and sure.

"On earth as it is in heaven" has been explained to me thus: In heaven, God's will is done as He speaks it; there is no lapse of time between what He desires and what is. I find myself in that place now, though still very much on earth; His presence is so completely with me, a part of me, that all His promises seem to be fulfilled with no time for them to be otherwise. I begin to stumble, and before I've fully realized that I'm stumbling, He is there, catching me, righting me, turning me back to the path. It's as if He's there to catch me BEFORE I start to fall. The whole time and space sequence seems irrelevant. I am. He is. We are.

That may be the essence of my new joy.

Child of God

*P*re-dawn, sleeping, I become aware of someone in my room. There is no sound that I can identify, but then I feel a small finger touching my shoulder. It doesn't prod or poke me, merely touches me gently. I realize my young daughter is standing beside my bed.

This happens every now and then; I really don't count how often it happens, though some people would. I accept it as part of our relationship, and our relationship is such a blessing to me that I don't even consider keeping track of how many times I've been wakened from sleep to find her there. I didn't keep up with it when she was an infant, either, when I had to wake up even more fully to find her, because she was too small to find me first. Of course it happened much more frequently then, so most of the time I simply kept her in the bed with me in those days, so that when she woke I would already be there. Now, she wakes up alone in her own bed in another room, and when she needs me, she gets up and walks to me. She is older now, more mature, stronger, and it is appropriate that she should do the walking. I keep nightlights in the bedrooms, bathrooms, hallways, so that she can find me, even in the dark. If she were to wake alone and afraid or hurt and should call out, though, I would hear her and wake even from the deepest sleep to go to her and meet her need. It's what I do for love; it's what love has made of me.

She used to have a sort of repeated "excuse" for coming to my bed. She would say something like, "Momma, can I sleep with you? I had a bad dream and I can't go back to sleep"; every night the same words in the same rhythm. She often would just tap the bed rather than touch me. I'd wake and ask whether she wanted to talk about the dream, and she never did. I would say that dreams go away when we wake up, and that she was awake and safe with me. I would pray aloud a prayer of comfort and rest for her. Then we'd fall asleep in each other's arms.

As it happened this morning, when I became aware of her finger on my shoulder, I turned over toward her while speaking to her, just as she started to ask if she could get in bed beside me. "Hi, Sweetie. You don't ever even have to ask. I am so glad you're here with me. Here, lie down, right here. Here's my cover. Are you warm enough?" She murmured assent and we held each other and drifted blissfully back to sleep. How blessed I am to have this delightful human being who comes to me for comfort and reassurance. What a joy simply to have her here where I am, to be able to kiss her hair and stroke her face, hold her close and feel her little hands rubbing my arm or back or side.

Before I was fully asleep in the darkened room, His light shone on me once again and showed me the image from His point of view. I wake up sometimes, from a dream or a daze or a time of distraction from Him. I find myself alone and exposed and uncomfortable. I make the trip to His side, walking through the darkness by the lights He has left for me. Uncertain of my position, not sure why I'm here or whether it's okay to ask for help again this time, I touch the hem of His garment or dare to lay a finger on His shoulder or hand. I repeat prayers, the same phrases that I've used so many times to excuse my entrance into His presence, even though no excuse is required. He doesn't have to wake up or turn to me, for He never slumbers, and He is always watching over me. Instead, as I did this morning, He says, "Hi, Sweetie. You don't ever even have to ask. I am so glad you're here with me. Here, lie down, right here. Here's my cover. Are you warm enough?" He wraps me in His grace and I am once again warm and safe and comforted. He lets me rest for as much timeless time as I need, and when I again open my eyes to look outward, the darkness is gone and all is bathed in His glorious light. He sends me out again, to play, to work, to be the delightful human being He made me to be, and He delights in me.

"Behold, what manner of love the Father hath bestowed upon us, that we should be called the sons of God . . ." (1 John 3:1).

What manner of love, indeed.

Propitiation

Propitiation. It's one of those words you almost never hear outside of church, and you wonder what it means when you hear it there. I've been hearing it a lot lately, as I've been studying in 1 John, and the concept is important to the understanding of the love of God John describes to us.

Propitiation. It is more than atonement; atonement is the payment for our sin, the death that secures life, the blood on the judgment seat that changes it to the mercy seat. Atonement satisfies the judgment, the wrath of God, by offering death as the penalty for sin. Propitiation goes beyond that. It removes the sin and secures the *favor* of God. Because Christ is the propitiation for our sin, God can look upon us not simply as paid up, with our sin accounts balanced. He looks upon us as holy and acceptable.

I cannot comprehend it. My heart swells, my mind expands, my eyes widen, and still I cannot take it all in. The love, the infinite and impossible love that He has shown to us in giving Himself so that we could be received; it is too much.

I see my own life. I see the filth I collected to cover myself, to hide from His revealing light. I see the pain that came into my life, that I thought was meant to destroy me. I see the shame of nakedness, of believing I was always seen by Him in my ugliness and sin and degradation.

Yet I am not there any more, and He sits beside me as I look at it all, holding my hand and waiting until I can hear His voice. He knows I cannot take all this in, so he gives me little pictures, little notes that I can understand.

He shows me now, after my tears of repentance and sorrow have stopped flowing, after I am able to be still and know. Shining His light again from another angle, He reveals that He used my feeble attempts to appear righteous. He took them and did even more than I had hoped, because He saw, all along, my heart. He does not see as men see; He does not see as I see. I was trying to make myself acceptable to Him, failing to believe that His work had already accomplished that on my behalf. Because He saw my heart, however, He counted even my self-righteousness as a cry for help, rather than an insult to His character.

What manner of love is this?

Yet, I understand. I am able to hear in my children's voices the cry for help, even when to other ears it may sound like a murmur of rebellion, a snarl of anger, a whimper of despair. I see the good in them, the hope, the potential, and I know with the right touch they can be made whole and stronger. I know this because I have been damaged, and He has touched me and made me whole.

Again I realize that every pain that has come into my life has been used of God to make me more whole, more complete, more pleasing to Him and to myself.

My heart – O God, thank you that my heart has ever been tuned to You, seeking You, longing for You, and that You have been able to do this amazing work in me.

He turned my filth into a filter.

I cannot say how, for His works are beyond my comprehension, but He took my pain, my sorrow, my fear, my shame, my ignorance, and wove them with His love into a filter through which truth has come to my children in a purer way than it otherwise could have reached them. I was determined that no one should have to bear what I had borne, that no one should face the condemnation I continually faced. I worked tirelessly to be sure my children understood their position before God. Continually I spoke truth to them, to be sure they comprehended not only their need for a Savior but their absolute acceptance by the Holy God who made them – even while I could not accept myself. Over and over I affirmed them in their uniqueness, not willing that any of them should ever think he was in any way flawed; instead, I determined that each of them should see his infinite worth and beauty as God sees. This I did, even as I continually fell short of my own expectations and never seemed to measure up fully to what I thought I was intended to be. Even when I could not see clearly myself, I trusted, I supported, I encouraged. I held back the flow of criticism and of judgment that inevitably comes from a world that views excellence as a target to destroy.

Now I see my children walking in that confidence that I worked so hard to ensure. One is heading a ministry, even while in military training in college. One is placed as a light in a very dark place, and his light has not dimmed. One is speaking his faith to believers much older than he and challenging them to deeper understanding. One is studying, taking notes, learning and applying deep principles of Scripture to life as a twelve-year-old. And one is speaking truth from a pure heart and revealing the simple beauty of God's message to us, understandable to a girl of seven years.

How blessed I would be if this were all, and yet there is more. He used my filth to make a filter, yes, and that allowed my children to see His holiness more clearly. He has gone beyond that to bless me directly, though. He has now taken that filter and shaken out all my contributions to its structure – all the things I did to try to make myself acceptable to Him. He has returned to me simply the love that held it all together.

Now I can see myself as He sees me. I can hear His voice without its being muffled by my own. And my children don't need the filter any longer, because they can see and hear as well.

This, then, is propitiation, in one little family in this corner of the world. Jesus took my sin, my shame, and my feeble attempts to please Him, because that was all I had to offer. He died to pay the penalty for my sin, then used all my flawed efforts to accomplish His perfect purposes in and through me, so that I could stand before a holy God unashamed, accepted, approved, forever. He even extended the blessing through me to my children.

What manner of love? Even this little picture is more than I can take in, really. What an awesome God we serve.

> And can it be that I should gain
> An interest in the Savior's blood?
> Died He for me, who caused His pain—
> For me, who Him to death pursued?
> Amazing love! How can it be
> That Thou, my God, shouldst die for me?
> Amazing love! How can it be
> That Thou, my God, shouldst die for me?
>
> 'Tis mystery all: th'Immortal dies:
> Who can explore His strange design?
> In vain the firstborn seraph tries
> To sound the depths of love divine.
> 'Tis mercy all! Let earth adore,
> Let angel minds inquire no more.
> 'Tis mercy all! Let earth adore,
> Let angel minds inquire no more.

He left His Father's throne above
So free, so infinite His grace—
Emptied Himself of all but love,
And bled for Adam's helpless race:
'Tis mercy all, immense and free,
For O my God, it found out me!
'Tis mercy all, immense and free,
For O my God, it found out me!

Long my imprisoned spirit lay,
Fast bound in sin and nature's night;
Thine eye diffused a quickening ray—
I woke, the dungeon flamed with light;
My chains fell off, my heart was free,
I rose, went forth, and followed Thee.
My chains fell off, my heart was free,
I rose, went forth, and followed Thee.

Still the small inward voice I hear,
That whispers all my sins forgiven;
Still the atoning blood is near,
That quenched the wrath of hostile Heaven.
I feel the life His wounds impart;
I feel the Savior in my heart.
I feel the life His wounds impart;
I feel the Savior in my heart.

No condemnation now I dread;
Jesus, and all in Him, is mine;
Alive in Him, my living Head,
And clothed in righteousness divine,
Bold I approach th'eternal throne,
And claim the crown, through Christ my own.
Bold I approach th'eternal throne,
And claim the crown, through Christ my own.

Charles Wesley, 1738

God Is Love

"God is love." 1 John 4:8

I heard a fantastic sermon this morning on the above text. One concept from the sermon has opened my mind to a new understanding of God and of belonging to Him.

Quoting C. S. Lewis, the speaker said that the phrase "God is love" implies the Trinity and the love and fellowship within God. Love cannot exist without an object. If God is love and He existed before creation, there must be giving and receiving of love within Him. My mind took off from there.

God invites us literally into that inclusive fellowship. When we are adopted into the family of God, we are adopted into God Himself. We partake of the eternal and ever-present communion with the self-existent One. All of life becomes worship. All that we do, because we do it in His presence and with Him, becomes holy, able to bless the world and also able to bless us by revealing to us more of who He is and who we are in Him.

I listen, holding my daughter's head in my lap, because this morning she needs my touch. How can she ever begin to comprehend the love God wants to lavish on her if I do not live it out with her? If her need, so obvious to her, goes unmet? If I see it but disparage it? Some would say, "She's nearly eight years old; she's too big to be held in church." Well, guess what? I'm a lot bigger than eight years old, and

I need to be held quite often. And I can testify to the pain of need unfulfilled. So why would I pass that on to my daughter?

I sit, stroking her hair, helping her to be comfortable lying on the seat and my lap. Holding her, I sense changes in her posture and position, and I am ever watchful for her ease and security. I lean forward to hear her whispered questions, her softly spoken concerns, and I answer her as completely as I can, explaining her uncertainties, affirming her understandings.

Is this any different from what God does for me? I think not. His continual attentiveness to my every need is evidence enough that He is continually watching me with rapt attention, constantly committed to helping me be sure of who I am and where I am and what is happening to me. I always have His ear, and He answers me sometimes before I am able to speak, because as He holds me ever in His hand He can tell what is troubling me even before I can. He senses the changes in my spirit and helps me to adjust, to understand, to stay close to Him.

I want to be the best parent I can be, to model love to my children in the best possible way so that they can have the best possible framework for beginning to understand His love. I want them to know that they can always come to me with any problem or need, and that I will always answer them as fully as possible or help them find the answers they seek. This is how I relate to God, and I know that we relate to God partly based on how we relate to our earthly parents. So, in addition to being grateful for parents who modeled love to me, I am very conscious of my sacred responsibility to show my children the love of God so that they, too, can relate to Him in a committed, trusting, open, intimate way.

When I come before God in the freedom of His love, partaking fully of the benefits of membership in His family,

Deborah L.W. Roszel

I come just as I am. I come without anything to recommend me except that I am responding to His direct invitation. I come boldly to the throne, into the very presence of the Three-in-One. I come, leaving behind all my pretenses and defenses, bringing my cares and concerns, my joys and hopes, and I pour them all out at His feet. He gazes at me, and I bask in the warmth of His smile, naked and unashamed in the assurance and acceptance of His love toward me.

This is love. This is God. And this is mine.

Thank you, Jesus.

Letting Go

$\mathcal{I}$ remember this little girl. She wanted the world to be perfect. Watch her playing. Everything orderly, everything clean. Neat rows. Careful labels.

I was a little girl once, and in some ways I still am. I still wonder at the beauty of creation. I still love running free and being surprised. I still find joy in flowers, bugs, sunshine, and kittens. I'm still afraid of things I don't understand.

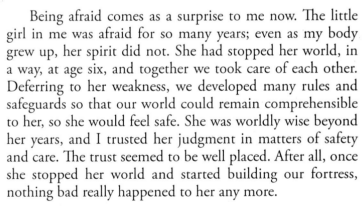

Being afraid comes as a surprise to me now. The little girl in me was afraid for so many years; even as my body grew up, her spirit did not. She had stopped her world, in a way, at age six, and together we took care of each other. Deferring to her weakness, we developed many rules and safeguards so that our world could remain comprehensible to her, so she would feel safe. She was worldly wise beyond her years, and I trusted her judgment in matters of safety and care. The trust seemed to be well placed. After all, once she stopped her world and started building our fortress, nothing bad really happened to her any more.

I'd almost forgotten that she was the reason we lived in a fortress. For that matter, I'd stopped noticing that we were in a fortress for much of the time. It was simply my world, my safe place. I understood everything. I followed the rules. I made sure others did as well, as much as possible. I feared those who did not.

Then everything changed, the fortress came down, I found myself in a Garden with no safety rails, and the little girl inside me was nowhere to be seen. No wonder. She was probably terrified, hiding under a chair somewhere. She does not trust wide open spaces even though they beckon to her temptingly; she does not go anywhere without safety rails, even though she wishes she could.

Since then, though, she's come around occasionally. She came and sang with me in church one morning when we were singing a favorite song of hers. She held my hand and skipped one afternoon when no one was watching and we decided that we didn't care even if they were. She laughed and played with me at the zoo when people *were* watching, but we were simply being ourselves, and it was wonderful. Now and then, she whispers to me of her fear, which still surrounds her and keeps her hiding much of the time.

We've been playing together in this Garden now for some time. I've been enjoying the freedom to grow, to stretch, to become whole, but she has not been quite so sure. The Garden is a pretty place for her, but she knows that pretty things must be treated with care. Special clothes, special shoes, special toys must be kept put away, only taken out for special days. She wonders how every day can be a special day.

How indeed? How can any day be a special day, when she must be ever on guard, ever watchful, ever vigilant? How can any real joy come to a six-year-old girl who is alone, afraid, hurt, and unsure of where to go for help? How can this child play in a Garden at all? She might get dirty. She might step on a plant. She might pick the wrong flower. She might eat the wrong fruit.

It happened to Eve. She ate the wrong fruit, and everything in the whole wide world turned dark because of her. It could happen to us. What if I eat the wrong fruit, the forbidden fruit? How will I know which fruit is forbidden with no signs or rails? Better not to eat at all, she reasons. Better not to venture into this danger-filled pretty place.

But we can't go back! Literally, there is nowhere to go back to. The fortress where we lived has been destroyed. The walls and rails we'd built for safety are no more. Love brought us out of there; love loosed our chains and destroyed our prison.

It freed us and then abandoned us, she reasons. Some love. She's seen that before, the abandonment, the demands to be strong, be grown up, be brave. She's begun to whisper to me more frequently of her concern. The longer we're out here, the less sure she is. She wants to find a safe, close place; everything here is open. The wind speaks to her of possible threats; the lushness of the Garden may hide danger; every change in the light startles her. Wise as she is, she is still only a child, and there is simply too much going on here for her to take in, and because it is all out of her control, it terrifies her. She really needs a hug and a nap.

I can hug her, hold her, carry her, but I cannot find a place that would suit her for a nap. There are no closed places here, no places where we cannot be seen. There is nowhere for a frightened child to hide, because this Garden was not made for frightened children. Fright was not part of the plan. But surely the One who made this Garden, who placed me here so intentionally, surely He knew the fear would come with me. What, then, is the plan?

To . . . grow . . . up?

To . . . I don't even know what that means. I am an adult. What does that mean? Stretching is good for me? Being vulnerable is part of being open? I get that, but she doesn't. Open is not part of her plan, and vulnerable is the one thing she never wants to be again. And no, I will not abandon her here. I am not moving another inch until this is clear to me. Hasn't she been through enough? Now, tell me where I am supposed to bring this child to have some rest. She has been awake for much too long, she has seen much too much, she is afraid and she needs a safe place.

"Give her to Me."

I . . . can't.

"You can."

No, I can't. She's mine. She's . . . she's me. How can I give that to You? What will I have left?

"Trust Me."

I can't.

"You can't? You can't trust Me?"

Okay, You're right. I'm the one who's afraid. Fine. Right. A grownup scared of a flower patch. Well, that's the way it is. Okay?

"Okay."

And yes, I'm the one who's hurting, too. A lot. Still. I just hadn't realized it, in so long. Um, could I just lie down here for a little while, and rest? I mean, I don't want to go away, and I really don't want to go back, but I just don't have the strength to go on right now.

"Then rest."

I can't rest. But I can't let her go.

I can hear her screams, the screams she never let out loud. She needs ME. I can't give her to You. She's afraid, can't You see? What will happen if I let go of her?

What if she . . .

Dies?

I . . . don't . . . think . . . I . . . can . . . handle . . . that.

I've never been alone, without her. She . . . we . . . take care of each other. I need HER.

"Rest."

The Holy One, the God of the Universe, is my Rock and my Redeemer. He is my strength in time of trouble. He is the One who makes me whole. Whole. Perfect. Complete. One.

You have drawn me to Your breast, Lord, to hear Your heart beating for me. You have invited me into the perfect fellowship of the Trinity, to be part of Your fullness that never ends, the love that is continually expressed in community among the Three in One. I am there, in Your midst.

Yes, You may have me, in all my manifestations. You may have me now, and in the future. You may have me in the past. You may have me as a broken, damaged six-year-old girl. And I trust You to restore, renew, redeem me, in every time, in every place, in every way.

Please, Lord, make me one.

Amen.

Waves

$\mathcal{I}$'m hearing echoes this morning, and I'm feeling them as well. They're like the waves on the lake, from the wake of a big boat going by too fast. Those waves can tip a kayak, and they threatened to tip me this morning. I'm not floating on the water, though, I'm standing in it, feet firmly planted, so the waves came by as a curiosity. They were enough to attract my notice, but not my concern.

Where did they come from? I don't see anything that could have caused them.

In the timelessness of time with God, He worked more on my healing yesterday. His work is so complete that the moment seems long ago now. Yesterday I gave Him something – someone – I'd been holding on to for forty-three years. That really seems like a long time, like forever. I can barely remember ever living without holding on to my six-year-old self to protect her and be protected by her.

Late last night just before falling asleep and early this morning just after waking, I heard her voice. Again, because of the way God finishes His work, her voice didn't even sound familiar to me; it was faint and from far away, but it had enough force to disturb my thoughts. It had an urgent sound to it, not to be ignored, and I responded appropriately. Someone needed me to pay attention to something, somewhere. I stopped what I was doing, both times, to try to pay attention – but there was nothing to see.

Nothing to have caused the voice of warning, nothing to have stirred the water.

Was that my Friend directing my attention to something He needs me to see? I pondered. I thought. I prayed. I listened. Because I do know His voice now, because it is ever-present with me, I realized that it was not His voice warning me. But I knew He did want my attention and had used this voice to accomplish that so He could speak to me.

There are ways of being that I had adopted in my relationship with my younger self. We had adopted patterns of response that were designed to reduce risk, ensure safety, and always protect us from exposure and harm. Yesterday, though, when I gave myself more fully to Him, specifically allowing Him to take my six-year-old self once and for all, He also took away the need to behave in that way.

I am no longer a small child in a terrifying world. I am no longer protecting a small child from harm. I am no longer listening to a small child's fears to inform my decisions about how to be and how to behave.

I did not expect this feeling of freedom from handing a child over to another's care. On the front side of that transaction, I was tearful and frightened, for her and for me. During the night God showed me the parallels between what happened yesterday and the times I left my own children in the care of another. Sometimes it brought tears to my eyes to let them go and to walk away, even if they weren't upset by the situation. The longing to be together is so strong; it is part of the price of love. But there was always someone there to say, "He'll be fine. We're going to have lots of fun. You need this break. Go take care of you." And that someone was always right.

So this feeling of freedom is not new to me, since God has allowed me to experience it before. He is the one caring for my children, anyway; He allows me to do His work most of the time, but there are definitely times when He calls me off that job to do another, or to be elsewhere, and He has other loving hands in place to do the work in my children's lives. Now I've had to give up not only part of my family but part of myself, and I have given myself to the care of the most perfectly loving hands of all – His. So there is no need for tears or for fear.

After dropping off the children for a few hours or even an overnight stay, I've found myself surprised to notice all sorts of feelings that I'd forgotten or never known were there. That's why all the parenting books say that parents should make a regular habit of going out as a couple, or moms should regularly go out alone or with friends. We need those times of being ourselves apart from our children. I can't say that I've done a good job of taking that advice regularly, but when I have, it has been beneficial to me and to my children.

Now, because my Friend is caring for the six-year-old who has been my sole charge for all these years, I find myself in a similar position, finding feelings that are completely new to me; although they have surely been around all along, I'd never been able to acknowledge them because I was caring for a six-year-old and filtering everything through her understanding and ability to cope. Suddenly, at forty-nine, I find myself able to be . . . an adult.

That's funny.

It is, and my Friend's twinkling eyes show His amusement at my discovery. He raises an eyebrow, smiles and nods as I go through my list of realizations. I don't have to run and hide when I'm afraid; I can simply say so and change my situation. I don't have to plan every word I speak or every move I make to accommodate the understanding and abilities of a child. I don't have to be embarrassed about feeling "adult" feelings or doing "adult" things; I don't have to behave as if a child is watching me all the time. I don't have to apologize for something I do that may not make sense to someone, or to me; I can simply figure it out and move on. I don't have to color everything in black and white, laying blame at the feet of at least one party in every disagreement between people. I don't have to assign guilt at all.

I think I could get used to this. I know I'd like to try.

When those waves come back by, as I'm sure they will, I'm not going to look for the source next time. I'm not going to jump out of the water and wait for it to settle before going back in. Instead, I'm going to look up, straight to the ultimate Source, and get the lowdown.

About the Author

Deborah Roszel has been accused of thinking too much, but it hasn't stopped her from studying and taking notes on a wide variety of subjects. She's an avid reader of novels, textbooks, Bibles, essays, treatises, legal documents, and cereal boxes. She earned a B.A. in Psychology from Furman University; after marriage, she and her husband, Rich, developed their very own experimental group of five children.

Deborah has learned from Southern Baptist, Presbyterian (PCA and USA), Episcopal, Anglican, and non-denominational Christian teachers. She has shared her love of learning with her children and many of their friends, teaching and tutoring in most every subject area as a homeschooler, classroom teacher, and private tutor.

With a broad theological and educational background, Deborah is still able to approach matters of faith as a seeker, aware that all interpretations of the supernatural are necessarily limited: we all have it wrong some of the time, She hopes that, some of the time, she might have it right.

Lightning Source UK Ltd.
Milton Keynes UK
UKOW03f2221230317
297349UK00002B/21/P